The Industrial Revolution

Manufacturing a Better America

Titles in *The American Saga* series

The Industrial Revolution

Manufacturing a Better America

R. Conrad Stein

 Enslow Publishers, Inc.
40 Industrial Road
Box 398
Berkeley Heights, NJ 07922
USA

http://www.enslow.com

Library of Congress Cataloging-in-Publication Data

Stein, R. Conrad.
    The Industrial Revolution: manufacturing a better America /
    R. Conrad Stein.
        p. cm. — (The American saga)
    Includes bibliographical references and index.
    ISBN 0-7660-2571-3
    1. Industrial revolution—United States—Juvenile literature. 2. Industrial
    revolution—Juvenile literature. I. Title. II. Series.
    HC105.S75 2006
    330.973'05—dc22

                                        2005027233

Printed in the United States of America

10 9 8 7 6 5 4 3 2 1

To Our Readers:
We have done our best to make sure all Internet Addresses in this book were
active and appropriate when we went to press. However, the author and the
publisher have no control over and assume no liability for the material available
on those Internet sites or on other Web sites they may link to. Any comments or
suggestions can be sent by e-mail to comments@enslow.com or to the address on
the back cover.

Illustration Credits: ©Corel Corporation, pp. 8, 30, 116 (bottom);
©Fujifotos/The Image Works, p. 111; Hemera Technologies, Inc., pp. 15,
100, 114 (top), 117 (bottom); The Library of Congress, pp. 3, 6, 10, 37, 45,
54, 65, 73, 75, 76, 78, 81, 85, 88, 92, 105, 107, 115, 116 (top), 117 (top), 118;
©Mary Evans Picture Library/The Image Works, p. 34; ©Michael
Wolf/VISUM/The Image Works, p. 113; Photos.com, pp. 56, 99; Smithsonian
Images, pp. 40, 41, 51, 97; ©SSPL/The Image Works, pp. 16, 22, 48, 114
(bottom); Stanford University Museum, p. 9; ©Steven Rubin/The Image
Works, p. 112; ©Topham/The Image Works, pp. 17, 43; United States Air
Force, p. 108.

Cover Illustration: The Library of Congress

Contents

Workers, railroad tycoons, and locals gather around as the last spike is about to be struck to join the Central Pacific and Union Pacific lines. Together the two lines would make the first transcontinental railroad—a product of the Industrial Revolution.

The Meeting of the Rails

May 10, 1869. On a dusty plain in Utah two railroad companies prepared to lay the final section of track for the transcontinental railroad. This railroad was destined to work miracles. Passengers could now ride a train from New York to San Francisco. For the first time the United States would be linked by iron rails from sea to shining sea.

The Utah meeting spot was called, for the occasion, Promontory Point. For three years crews had toiled to build the great railroad. Men of the Central

Telegraph operators were poised to flash the news to a waiting country.

Pacific started in California and worked east. Laborers of the Union Pacific began in Nebraska and proceeded west. Millions of spikes had been driven into miles of track to create this wondrous railroad line. Now newspaper writers and photographers stood ready to record the ceremonious driving of the last spike. Telegraph operators were poised to flash the news to a waiting country.

Leland Stanford, one of the owners of the Central Pacific, rose to drive the final spike home. Stanford was dressed in elegant clothes and wore a fancy top hat. As hundreds watched, he raised a sledgehammer over his head and swung it down. He missed the spike and hit a rail. Workers watching the event laughed uproariously. Despite the miss, a telegraph operator tapped out a single word: DONE. Through the miracle of the telegraph, the news flashed throughout the United States that the great railroad was completed at last.

Around the country parties burst to life. In New York City one hundred cannons were fired in a booming

The *119* was one of the steam engines at the Promontory Point celebration of the completion of the transcontinental railroad. A modern reconstruction of the locomotive is pictured.

salute. Chicagoans formed a parade that grew to seven miles long. In Sacramento, California, crews lined up thirty train engines decorated with blue and white paper. These colorful train engines blew their whistles together as if joined in song. The United States celebrated a marriage of sorts. The East was finally married to the West. Miles and miles of silver rails served as the wedding ring. The spike driven at Promontory Point represented the final kissing of the bride.

Railroads were perhaps the most exciting development in the United States and the rest of the world during the 1800s. Before railroads, most people never ventured more than fifty miles from where they were born. Then, in less than a lifetime, travel evolved from horse-drawn wagons to mighty locomotives speeding over iron rails.

The growth of railroads took place because of the Industrial Revolution. Normally the word "revolution" means a sudden and sometimes violent change. The Industrial Revolution lacked that speed and drama. Still, it was a great turning point in history. It erased an

The Golden Spike

A golden spike marked the finish of the transcontinental railroad. However, that high-priced spike did not stay in the rails. Instead, it was used only as a symbol of the great achievement. The golden spike hammered at Promontory Point on that historic day is now displayed at the Stanford Museum of Stanford University in Palo Alto, California.

old agricultural way of life and created a new society based on industrial production.

The Industrial Revolution was based upon machines entering the workplace. Machines did work that used to be done by hand. Therefore clothing and other everyday products were cheaper and more

In order to build the transcontinental railroad, teams of workers had to use dynamite to blast tunnels through the Rocky Mountains.

In 1803, when he was a young man, Patrick Gass hiked to the Pacific as a member of the Lewis and Clark Expedition. That team of explorers traveled roughly the same route that was later followed by the western half of the transcontinental railroad. Gass and the others spent a year and a half trekking from the Missouri River to the Pacific Coast. Riding the new railroad, first-class passengers made the same trip in about five days. Patrick Gass died in April 1870, at age ninety-nine. He was the last surviving member of the Lewis and Clark Expedition. Within his lifetime, the country and especially the West were transformed by the railroads.

accessible to most people. But the blessings came with pains. Factory hands worked long hours at repetitive tasks. Some people grew rich while the masses lived in poverty. Giant factories fouled rivers and polluted the air.

The results of the Industrial Revolution are debated to this day. Yet it would be impossible to feed the 6.2 billion people who live on the planet today without the aid of machines in agriculture. Though scholars and poets often decry the Industrial Revolution, we all live in the world it created. That world—often called the Machine Age—began in Great Britain more than two hundred years ago.

Great Britain: Mother of the Industrial Revolution

The introduction of the steam engine, and the spinning machine, added, in an extraordinary manner, to the powers of human nature . . . they have, in half a century, multiplied the productive power, or the means of creating wealth . . .[1]

Robert Owen (1771–1858), a textile mill owner who made a fortune during the early stages of the British Industrial Revolution.

In 1700, most people in Great Britain lived in farming communities. Farmers grew the food they needed for their families. If they were lucky, they had some surplus crops at the end of their harvest. They usually traded the extra food for products such as clothing, furniture, and iron pots and pans. Such goods were made in small local workshops or were brought by merchants from other towns. This way of life, that saw most people working the soil while a few produced goods, had continued more or less unchanged for hundreds of years.

Rarely did people starve under this farming system. But no one knew when drought or disease would ruin a harvest and bring hunger to a community. Only the royalty or the large landowners lived in relative comfort. Children of the wealthy were taught to read while the majority of farmers (peasants) could not even sign their names. It was almost impossible for a person to advance from the peasant class to the upper class.

However, the seeds of change were present in British society. Great Britain had a vast overseas colonial empire. Its prize colonies in North America would one day become the United States. Colonies gave the mother country a built-in market for manufactured goods. This meant that shop-produced items, such as farm tools and clothing, were relatively easy to sell to consumers in the colonies.

Also, Great Britain had something other nations in Europe lacked: a growing middle class. Most countries on the European continent had a huge number of peasants, a few wealthy landowners, and almost no one living in between. Great Britain, by contrast, nurtured well-to-do businessmen who had money to invest in shops and factories. This middle class grew because improvements in farming in the early 1700s brought more wealth to the land. Money that was readily available for investment was called "venture capital." Many budding businessmen decided to put their venture capital into the British clothing industry.

The Textile Revolution

The textile industry produces clothing, bed sheets, blankets, and other goods made from fabric. The manufacture of textiles marked the first great step in the Industrial Revolution. In fact, some historians claim the movement, in its earliest stages, ought to be called the Textile Revolution.

In the 1700s most clothing was made from woolen yarn or cotton thread. Cotton is a fibrous plant, which produces a natural thread as it grows. Yarn and thread were manufactured with the help of a machine called

Adam Smith, the Philosopher of Capitalism

Capitalism is an economic system in which people are allowed to buy and sell goods freely. The Scottish economist Adam Smith (1723–1790) is generally regarded as the first theorist of modern capitalism. In 1776, Smith published *The Wealth of Nations*. The book urged governments to allow free trade of goods and to promote the rights of individuals to invest money in projects such as shops and factories. This is the basis of the free enterprise system that capitalistic countries follow today. Smith argued that buyers and sellers seeking profit in an open market bring wealth to an entire nation. The investors enrich a nation without even knowing they are doing it—"as if by an invisible hand."

the spinning wheel. The spinning wheel was turned by a foot pedal or a hand crank. As the wheel spun, the operator guided thread into the moving parts. The parts twisted the threads together to create yarn. It was a slow process, which took many hours of labor to produce a few feet of yarn.

In Great Britain, "spinning" took place in individual homes. Neighborhoods or even whole towns worked as spinners. The production of yarn was known as a "cottage industry" because it was largely carried out in homes or cottages. Merchants used their venture capital to buy the yarn from spinners and sell it to weavers who made cloth. This method of producing textiles was changed forever when British inventors devised new machines.

Most homes in eighteenth-century Great Britain had a spinning wheel.

James Hargreaves (1720–1778) was a carpenter and a spinner who lived in the English village of Stanhill. One day, according to an often-told story, his daughter Jenny accidentally knocked over his spinning wheel. To their surprise the wheel still functioned even though it was on its side. This gave Hargreaves an idea: Why not use one wheel to take thread off of eight or even ten spindles? By using several spindles he could make yarn at a faster rate. In 1764, Hargreaves made what he called the spinning jenny. He named the machine for his daughter whose moment of clumsiness inspired his invention. Though James Hargreaves could not read or write, he was one of the great pioneers of the Industrial Revolution. By the time he died in 1778, thousands of spinning jennies were in use.

This is a replica of Hargreaves's original design for the spinning jenny.

Other British-made devices joined the spinning jenny to create a new and radically different textile industry. John Kay (1704–1780) conceived the flying shuttle which greatly speeded up the weaving of yarn into cloth. The water frame, developed by Sir Richard Arkwright (1732–1792), was a weaving machine that ran on water power. Samuel Crompton (1753–1827) created the spinning mule, which combined the features of the water frame and the spinning jenny.

Within twenty years, spinning and weaving ceased to be a cottage industry in England. Textile production moved from the cottages into large factories which employed hundreds of workers. With this new style of textile manufacturing, the Industrial Revolution was underway.

Change is never accepted easily. As new machines destroyed the old clothing industry, spinners and weavers rose up in rebellion. Mobs marched on the newly built factories and wrecked the textile machines. They believed the new machines were robbing them of their livelihood. In 1769, the British Parliament passed a law threatening the death penalty for anyone who damaged a machine. Still, the protests continued. The most aggressive of the machine-wreckers were the Luddites, who emerged in 1811. No one is certain of the origin of their name. Some say they followed a made-up monarch called King Ludd. The Luddites attacked textile mills from Nottingham to Lancaster in a rebellion that lasted two years.

The Luddites often rioted, destroying machines throughout Great Britain.

Steam and Iron

Before the Industrial Revolution, workers powered machines with wind (windmills) and with rushing rivers (waterwheels). Animals such as horses and mules were also employed to provide power. Machinery in pre-industrial times often drove grinding stones which ground wheat grains into flour.

Curious minds pondered another source of power—steam. It had always been known that steam bubbling out of a pot of boiling water generated enough force to rattle the pot's lid. More than two thousand years ago, Greek craftsmen built devices that rotated by the power of steam. Those early machines were little more than curiosities. It was not until the Industrial Revolution that steam power was used on a grand

Curious minds pondered another source of power— steam.

scale in manufacturing and in transportation. Once more, the most significant early steam engines were invented in Great Britain.

Water seeping into coal mines posed a constant problem for miners. As early as 1698, an Englishman named Thomas Savery invented a steam-driven pump to remove the water from the floor of a mine. Another Englishman, Thomas Newcomen, improved on this pump with his own device in 1712. Newcomen's machine worked like a mechanical seesaw, and did a better job of draining water from mine shafts. The steam-powered pumps allowed miners of coal, copper, and tin to dig deep below the groundwater level and extract ores.

James Watt (1736–1819) worked as an instrument maker for the University of Glasgow in Scotland. The job was perfect for Watt, who loved to tinker with mechanical devices. As a boy he had been brilliant in the study of geometry. Watt examined existing steam engines, especially the pump designed by Thomas Newcomen. He determined that the seesaw-type pump was inefficient. Watt devised a steam-driven motor that turned a wheel. He did not invent the steam engine, but he vastly improved the device. His model required less coal to fire the boiler and therefore made steam power practical for industry.

New and more efficient steam engines were soon used to drive textile-making machines. The marriage of steam and spinning and weaving by machines produced clothing and textile products faster and more cheaply than ever before.

Steam-driven motors and textile-making machines were made of iron. This led to still another revolution in the iron industry. People made iron by heating iron ore in a furnace in

What's a Watt?

Today we are reminded of James Watt every time we screw a lightbulb into a socket. The power of a lightbulb is measured in watts, such as 40, 75, and 100. James Watt did not experiment with electricity. But his name is associated with power. Therefore units of electrical power are still named after the long-ago Scottish inventor.

a process called smelting. For ages, smelting furnaces were fired by wood. But Great Britain's hardwood forests were depleted by 1700. Once more, British inventors rose to the challenge. In the early 1700s, the Englishman Abraham Darby discovered how to burn coke to smelt iron. Coke was produced by burning coal. Great Britain was rich in coal deposits and soon became the world's leading iron-maker.

Industry created industry in the early stages of Britain's Industrial Revolution. Textile machines and steam engines were made from iron, and so the iron industry expanded. Coal was needed to make iron, and therefore coal mining grew. Iron products and coal had to be transported from place to place. To achieve efficient transportation, engineers dug England's great canal system. Cargo could now be shipped cheaply by canal boats.

Most historians regard the year 1760 as the official start of the Industrial Revolution in Great Britain. From its beginnings, the revolution swept the country and transformed the life of its people in just a few short decades.

A New Age

On a sunny day in May 1851, a huge crowd gathered in London's Hyde Park to attend a fair called the Great Exhibition. No one used the term Industrial Revolution at the time, but the Great Exhibition celebrated advances brought about by new and wondrous machinery. Men and women gaped at a high-speed printing press and a huge train engine. One newly invented home appliance, a gas cooking stove, drew great attention. All these mechanical marvels were undreamed of by the grandparents of those attending the fair.

In the center of the fairgrounds rose the Crystal Palace. This was a sprawling exhibit hall made from an iron frame inset with three hundred thousand panes of glass. The glass industry too had thrived in recent years. The Crystal Palace and the fantastic machinery it held stood as a testament to how science and invention had transformed the world. Prince Albert formally opened the fair by saying, "The Exhibition of 1851 is to give us a true test and a living picture of the point of development at which the whole of mankind has arrived . . ."[2]

The most famous person attending the Great Exhibition was Queen Victoria, Britain's monarch. She took the throne in 1837 at age eighteen and held it until her death in 1901. The time of her rule is called the Victorian Age. It coincided with Great Britain's transformation into the world's mightiest industrial nation. So many factories and railroads were built in the Victorian Age that Britain was hailed as the "workshop of the world."

Arnold Toynbee Gives the Movement a Name

The Industrial Revolution had already changed the world before it acquired its name. In 1884, the best-known book of British philosopher Arnold Toynbee (1852–1883) was published. *The Industrial Revolution*, which was largely critical of how workers suffered in the factory system of the time. Subsequent writers began calling the machine-driven age the Industrial Revolution.

The inside of the Crystal Palace boasted beautiful fountains and statues.

When the teenage Victoria became queen in 1837, 80 percent of the British people lived on farms. When she retired as queen sixty-three years later the numbers were reversed. By then, eight out of every ten British subjects were city dwellers.

The Industrial Revolution needed labor just as it needed coal and iron ore as raw material. For better or for worse, people left farmland and flooded into cities where they found jobs as factory hands. Factory buildings, with smokestacks belching fumes, rose in Birmingham, Sheffield, Manchester, Leeds, Glasgow, and scores of other cities and towns. The agricultural way of life, unchanged in Great Britain for hundreds of years, was soon replaced by a new order ruled by cities and industries.

The mass migration of workers from the farms resulted in cities which were miserably overcrowded. In England's industrial centers, families lived eight or ten people to a room. Makeshift housing to accommodate the crush of new city dwellers included basements, attics, or converted barns. Sanitation in the slums was deplorable. Sewers were open trenches running down the middle of the streets. Toilets were nonexistent. Killer diseases, such as cholera and typhus, raged through the slum sections. In some industrial towns, almost half the children born to the working class died before they reached adulthood.

Factories were dark, dirty places where hundreds of workers stood over benches and machines to perform their tasks. Textile mills preferred women as factory

"A Squalid Neighborhood"

The British novelist Charles Dickens (1812–1870) was a popular writer and a stern social critic of his time. Dickens was born into an impoverished family and knew the slums from firsthand experience. In one of his most famous novels, *Oliver Twist*, his leading character walks through an area the author calls "a squalid neighborhood:"

> *Some houses which had become insecure from age and decay, were prevented from falling into the street, by huge beams of wood reared against the walls, and firmly planted in the road; but even these crazy dens seemed to have been selected as the nightly haunts for some houseless wretches. . . . The very rats, which here and there lay putrefying in its rottenness, were hideous with famine.*[3]

hands because they were skilled at sewing and would work for lower wages than men expected. Also, women were less likely to join unions to demand higher wages.

Men and women commonly worked twelve- to fourteen-hour shifts. Toil was monotonous, with workers performing the same movements over and over again. Wages provided little more than bare necessities of food and rent. Many employers had a low opinion of their workers. They believed wages must be kept low because only hunger would force working-class men and women to return to their machines.

Child labor was one of the great injustices imposed on the lower classes. An official report written in 1843 claimed, "that instances occur in which Children begin to work as early as three or four years of age . . . in general, regular employment commences between seven and eight . . ."[4] Many children who worked in mills and coal mines lived in dormitories and suffered conditions similar to those found in the worst jails. In 1832, a judge questioned a child textile-mill worker named Peter Smart. "Do the children ever attempt to run away?" asked the judge. "Very often," Peter Smart answered. "Did you ever attempt to run away?" "Yes, I ran away twice." "And you were brought back?" "Yes; and I was sent up to the master's loft, and thrashed with a whip for running away."[5]

The great dilemma of the Industrial Revolution lies in the mixed blessings it produced. In England the sudden shift from hand labor to machinery left many people in wretched poverty. Yet others enjoyed middle-class status or even fabulous wealth. Women were liberated by factory jobs, but they were also enslaved by low wages and long hours. Children were sent to toil in factories and mines. Still, England's school system expanded dramatically as the country industrialized.

A middle class thrived in the same urban centers crowded with poor people. In those days, middle-class men wore formal black suit coats to work. The "black-coats" included merchants, shopkeepers, bankers, and clerks. Factories needed engineers. British universities expanded to train engineers and managers, most of whom came from the middle class. Democracy grew as a stronger force in the industrialized British society. The Great Reform Act of 1832 doubled the number of people who were eligible to vote in Great Britain.

The House of Commons, one of the two houses in the British Parliament, soon was dominated by members elected by middle-class voters.

The voice of reform rose amid the horrors of the Industrial Revolution. Labor unions had long been forbidden by law in Great Britain. Despite the law, workers met secretly to try to win better wages and job conditions from their bosses. In 1824, the British Parliament made labor unions legal. Parliament passed the Factory Act in 1833, which regulated child labor.

Great Britain rose to become the world's wealthiest country due largely to its leadership in the Industrial Revolution. Most of this wealth was concentrated in the hands of the upper classes. Still, workers made great strides too. Historians often cite the inequities of life during Britain's industrialization period—slums, poverty, and child labor. But no one denies that the late 1700s and the 1800s were a time of immense progress and growing democracy.

The Industrial Revolution spread from Great Britain to Belgium, France, and Germany. Wherever it went, the new machine-driven culture altered the people's way of life. In the early 1800s, the revolution crossed the Atlantic Ocean and made its impact on the United States.

American Industrialization

In the late eighteenth century America began not one revolution but two. The American War of Independence coincided with the advent of American industrialization . . .[1]

Professor John F. Kasson, writing in 1976, is a cultural historian at the University of North Carolina.

The Beginnings

On a hot summer day in July 1778, General George Washington and his top assistant, Alexander Hamilton, had lunch in a country spot that is now Paterson, New Jersey. As they ate they gazed at a spectacular sight—the Great Falls of the Passaic River. The American War of Independence was raging. Washington no doubt worried about his next battle with the British army. But Hamilton looked at the thundering waterfall and thought of it as a source of power. He later proposed that an industrial city be built around this waterfall. The rushing water would drive turbines for mills and factories. Workers would live in cottages near the factory buildings.

The United States won its War of Independence against Great Britain. The Treaty of Paris (1783) officially ended the war and established the United States as a new and independent nation.

Alexander Hamilton (1755–1804) became the first secretary of the treasury of the United States. He was a powerful figure in the early years of the U.S. government. Hamilton was also a visionary in gauging the future of his country's economy. He saw a time when the United States would develop big business and manufacturing enterprises. In 1791, Hamilton issued his Report on Manufactures that called on the federal government to encourage the growth of factories.

At the time of independence, Hamilton held a minority view. The vast majority of Americans lived on farms in the late 1700s. There was little reason to believe this situation would change. Even the brilliant Thomas Jefferson, the country's third president, thought the United States would remain an agricultural society for generations to come.

Some American industry had developed even before independence. Shipbuilding was established in Massachusetts and Maine. Many rural areas produced whiskey. Small foundries engaged in iron making. But manufacturing in no way approached the scale it had reached in Great Britain. America's finest manufacturers were the blacksmiths who ran shops in the farming villages. The town blacksmith made all of their goods by hand. He made horseshoes and the nails he used to fasten the shoes to the horses' hooves. Blacksmiths even made their own hammers.

Historians disagree as to exactly when the Industrial Revolution started in the United States. Some point to an enterprising Englishman who built a textile mill. Others cite the threat of war and the work of an American mechanical genius.

Samuel Slater (1768–1835) was born in England. He worked in the textile industry with Sir Richard Arkwright, the inventor of the water frame. As a

War is often called "the mother of invention."

young man, Slater decided that the textile business was too competitive in Great Britain. He wanted to bring his skills to the United States. But the British textile industry jealously guarded its manufacturing techniques. Industrial leaders would not let experts such as Slater travel abroad. Slater fooled his bosses by boarding a ship dressed in the plain clothes of a young farmer. In 1790, Slater built machinery similar to that invented by Arkwright and opened a spinning mill in Pawtucket, Rhode Island. The mill was the first large factory to operate in the United States.

War is often called "the mother of invention." In warfare men need weapons. So, when the infant nation felt threatened by the wars raging in Europe at that time, it turned to a man who had a novel idea for

Paul Revere, Industrialist and Patriot

Though the infant United States had no factories, it did enjoy the works of master craftsmen. One such craftsman was the silversmith Paul Revere (1735–1818). Born in Boston, Revere fashioned marvelous teapots and sugar bowls made of silver. After the United States achieved independence, Revere expanded his operations. He made bronze plates for printing presses and bronze bells for church steeples. Paul Revere will always be best known for his heroic role as a patriot. On the night of April 18, 1775, he rode his horse down dark roads to warn fellow revolutionaries at Lexington and Concord that the British army was on the move. That courageous ride was immortalized one hundred years later by the poet Henry Wadsworth Longfellow in these well-known opening lines:

> Listen, my children, and you shall hear
> Of the midnight ride of Paul Revere,[2]

In this painting by John Singleton Copley, silversmith and patriot Paul Revere poses with one of his fine silver teapots.

the mass production of firearms. For centuries, guns, known as muskets, were made by hand. Each part of a musket was fashioned by a craftsman to fit that individual firearm. Eli Whitney (1765–1825) claimed he could make muskets faster and cheaper by using "interchangeable parts." He planned to make identical triggers, bolts, and other rifle workings by machine. Parts from one musket would always fit neatly into another. Making goods with interchangeable parts was a new concept in the early 1800s. Whitney won a government contract to make muskets, and he earned a fortune from making the weapons.

Between 1815 and 1850 American industry expanded at a rapid pace. Shipbuilding continued until the American merchant fleet became second only to that of the British. Mountainous New England states channeled their fast-flowing rivers into waterwheels to drive factory machinery. As was true in Great Britain, the textile business led the way. Textile mills operated in Fall River and Lowell, Massachusetts. Shoemaking factories appeared in the Massachusetts towns of Brockton, Haverhill, and Lynn. Waterwheels also powered sawmills which sliced logs into boards for building.

A new type of water-driven flour mill was invented by Oliver Evans (1755–1819). Born in Newport, Delaware, Evans worked in various mills as a teenager. During his off-hours he studied science, math, and engineering. In 1808, Evans built a steam-powered flour mill in Pittsburgh. The mill powered stones which in turn ground wheat grain into flour for bread-making. Evans also drew up plans for a high-pressure steam engine. This engine was lighter and smaller than the ones then in use. Evans even predicted the automobile when he wrote: ". . . the time will come when people will travel in stages [stagecoaches] moved by steam engines from one city to another, almost as fast as birds fly, fifteen or twenty miles per hour."[3]

Steam power added a new chapter to the Industrial Revolution. Early factories were driven by water-wheels and therefore had to be located beside rivers. Factories powered by steam engines could be built any-where. Steam engines were fired by coal, and the coal industry expanded too.

By the early 1800s, the United States was already a competitor with industrial England. During the 1851 Great Exhibition in London, an American-made farm implement called the McCormick reaper won in compe-tition with reapers made in European nations. Clocks, pianos, and other manufactured goods from the United States astounded the British public. The United States, once a backward British colony, had emerged as an industrial power.

The Industrial Revolution and the Westward Movement

Early in U.S. history, the vast majority of people lived on a sliver of land hugging the East Coast. Americans looked to the West as a region where they could build settlements and establish farms. But blocking westward expansion stood the Appalachian Mountains. The mountain chain rose like a jagged wall to pen the people into the eastern states.

The Cumberland Road, also called the National Road or the National Pike, was the first large-scale effort to cross the Appalachians. The road cut through

President Thomas Jefferson said talk of making such a canal, "is little short of madness."

the mountains at the Cumberland Gap in present-day Maryland. Eventually it wound five hundred miles through the forests to central Illinois. Work on the road began in 1811. The Cumberland Road could be called the nation's first superhighway.

The new Cumberland Road served farmers and pioneers who walked or took horses over its length. However, if industry were to develop in the West, heavy equipment must move through the Appalachians. In those days, canal boats could carry heavy loads cheaply and efficiently. But most experts thought it was impossible to dig a canal through the towering Appalachians. In the early 1800s, President Thomas Jefferson said talk of making such a canal, "is little short of madness."[4]

New York State Governor DeWitt Clinton (1769–1828) believed a westward canal was both practical and necessary for the future of the United States.

He wanted to build a canal that cut through the Appalachian Mountains and over the forests of upstate New York. Clinton persuaded the New York state legislature to vote funds for the project.

On July 4, 1817, work began on a project called the Erie Canal. When completed, almost eight years later, the canal connected Albany on the Hudson River to Buffalo on Lake Erie. An ingenious system of locks lifted canal boats up one side of mountains and down the other. The new waterway delivered passengers and heavy freight over the Appalachians and through the rugged lands of upstate New York.

The United States was laced with streams and rivers. Before the Industrial Revolution two kinds of

A boat leaves one of the Erie Canal's locks in 1910.

The Erie Canal Changes Life in Upstate New York

In all, the Erie Canal ran 363 miles over what were once forests and sleepy farmlands in New York State. Repair shops, hotels, restaurants, and entire new towns developed along the route. A canal culture grew too, as poems and songs were written about the great ditch. Canal boats were pulled by horses or mules which walked on a towpath alongside the canal banks. One of the most popular songs of the time celebrated a boat-towing mule:

I've got a mule, her name is Sal,
Fifteen miles on the Erie Canal.
She's a good old worker and a good old pal,
Fifteen miles on the Erie Canal.
We've haul'd some barges in our day,
Fill'd with lumber, coal and hay,
And we know ev'ry inch of the way
From Albany to Buffalo.[5]

riverboats took people and farm animals to the new lands in the West. The most common was the flatboat, used only for downriver trips. Flatboats were made from logs which were nailed together. When the downriver destination was reached the flatboat owner simply pulled the nails and dismantled the craft. The owner then put the nails in a sack, because they were valuable, and walked back upriver. A craft called a keelboat could travel upstream. Keelboats had crews of twenty or more muscular men. The men jabbed long poles into the river bottom and laboriously pushed the vessel upriver against the currents. Both flatboats and keelboats had severe limitations. Desperately needed was a powerboat. Such a boat could defy the river's flow and sail upstream as well as down without the need of excessive manual labor.

Steam engines in the United States were thought of as a source of stationary power. They were often too big to put into a boat. The American John Fitch briefly operated a steam-powered boat on the Delaware River in 1786, but his vessel failed to make money. It took a bold businessman named Robert Fulton to successfully bring steam power to American rivers.

Robert Fulton (1765–1815) was born on a farm in Pennsylvania. As a boy he showed enormous talent as an inventor. He made lead pencils and kitchen utensils for his mother. He fashioned fireworks, including sky-rockets, for a town party. Finally, he dedicated his life to building a practical steamboat. Backed by a wealthy investor named Robert Livingston, Fulton built a ship called the *Clermont*. Many people believed the vessel would sink on its first voyage. The boat was widely called "Fulton's Folly." Fulton fooled all of his critics. On August 17, 1807, the *Clermont* made its first voyage. It steamed up the Hudson River from New York City to Albany. The boat carried passengers and was an immediate success. Fulton even served tea and cake to people traveling on his boat.

Steamboats appeared on the Ohio and Mississippi rivers. St. Louis, Louisville, and New Orleans became major river ports. The Mississippi and Ohio rivers turned into highways to the West. Steamboats burned

A replica of Robert Fulton's *Clermont* gets ready to steam up the Hudson River during a 1909 celebration of Fulton's historic achievement.

The Golden Age of Sail

For more than two thousand years people built sailing ships to carry goods and passengers over the seas. In the early 1800s, American shipbuilders developed the fastest line of oceangoing sailing ships that ever took to the waters. They were the tall, sleek clipper ships. These marvelous vessels were built in Baltimore, Boston, and New York. Clippers brought tea from China. They took prospectors around Cape Horn at the tip of South America, and brought them up to the gold fields in California. More than 150 years ago, clipper ships raced across the Atlantic in just two weeks. Clippers were gorgeous vessels whose beauty inspired poets and painters. Their owners gave the magnificent ships romantic names—the *Rainbow*, the *Sea Witch*, the *Flying Cloud*, the *Westward Ho*, and the *Lightning*.

The reign of the clipper was glorious but short. From 1850 to 1870 the clippers, most of which were made in America, ruled the seas. Soon, steam engines were fitted to oceangoing vessels. Steamships were dependable and could make their way over the seas whether there was wind or no wind. One by one, the magnificent clipper ships went to scrapyards. The only one remaining is the *Cutty Sark*, a British-built clipper. The *Cutty Sark* is displayed today in London for ship-lovers to see and admire. The Industrial Revolution brought steam to the ocean. In the process, it ended the era of the clipper ship, which has been called the Golden Age of Sail.

either wood or coal to fire a boiler. The boilers produced high-pressure steam which drove huge paddle wheels. Puffing like giant teakettles, the steamboats quickly replaced the old flatboats and keelboats in America's inland waterways.

Telegraphs and Trains

Communications between American cities were once limited to letters and newspapers delivered by slow stagecoaches. When people in western states such as Missouri voted in presidential elections, they had to wait three weeks or more to find out which candidate had won. The daring horseback riders of the pony express sped mail to the far western states, but this was an expensive process. The pony express lasted less than two years, from April 1860 to October 1861.

Communications within the United States were revolutionized by the development of the telegraph. The almost miraculous "talking wires" transferred messages instantaneously over hundreds of miles.

Samuel Morse (1791–1872) began his work life as a very talented artist. As a young man he traveled to Europe, where critics admired his paintings. However, few people bought his work. Morse spent many years as an impoverished artist. He was having dinner aboard a ship when he overheard a fellow diner say that scientists had learned how to send electricity through wires. In a burst of inspiration, Morse thought: Why not send messages long-distance through wires by electricity? Developing his idea required years of work without pay. This posed no great problem because Morse was accustomed to living the life of a starving artist.

On May 24, 1844, Morse strung a wire between Washington, D.C., and Baltimore. He announced he would demonstrate his new telegraph. The telegraph worked when a sender tapped out electrical currents over a wire. The sender used an electrical switch called a key. At the other end of the wire was an electromagnet.

This key was used to transmit messages through Morse's telegraph.

Current caused the electromagnet to pull down a bar and make a clicking noise. Morse devised a code. Short clicks (dots) and long clicks (dashes) formed words. As a large crowd watched, Morse tapped out what became a famous message: "What hath God wrought." Samuel Morse, the onetime starving artist, became a rich man through profits from his telegraph.

Steam locomotives moving on track were an English invention imported to the United States. A small steam-driven train was built in New Jersey as early as 1815. In 1830, a famous race was held near Baltimore. The race pitted a locomotive called the *Tom Thumb* against a horse pulling a wagon. The race began with *Tom Thumb* establishing a long lead. Then, toward the finish, the train's engine broke down and the horse won. Most people watching the race cheered for the horse. Spectators jeered at the puffing locomotive, calling it a "tea-kettle on a truck."[6] (In those days people often called a wagon a truck.) In the *Tom Thumb* race, a horse beat a steam-driven train. But this victory of animal power over steam power was short-lived.

By 1840, some three thousand miles of train track had been laid down in the country. Trains eclipsed many of the newly dug canals, driving them out of business. The Erie Canal, however, was well established and remained profitable despite competition from trains. Railroad tracks reached as far west as Chicago in 1848. In just ten years, Chicago became the nation's leading railroad center.

The *John Bull* made its historic first run in 1831 on the Camden and Amboy Railroad in New Jersey.

The Great Divide

The American Industrial Revolution began in the northeast and spread west. For the most part, factories and mills were concentrated in the northern states. Thus a great divide began to emerge in the country. The North developed a mixed economy of small farms and industry while the South remained largely agricultural.

Eli Whitney has a dual role in the story of the American Industrial Revolution. He was the first to build muskets with interchangeable parts, and he made money on that enterprise. He also invented the cotton gin. Whitney earned very little on his invention, but he was given a curious place in history. The cotton gin brought new life to an evil institution—slavery.

Taking a job as a private tutor, Eli Whitney traveled to Georgia in 1793. There he saw slaves working by hand at the painstaking task of separating the tough little seeds from raw cotton. He had never seen raw cotton before. He was shocked at how difficult it was to process the material. Whitney wrote to his father that, ". . . if a machine could be invented [to clean out the seeds] it would be a great thing both to the Country and the inventor."[7]

The prospect of creating such a machine excited Whitney's inventive mind. In just ten days he designed and built the first cotton gin. The machine was amazingly simple. It used a hand-cranked cylinder with rows of teeth to comb out the seeds as it turned. The gin's ability to clean cotton was astounding. Cotton production soared on southern farms. For Whitney, the

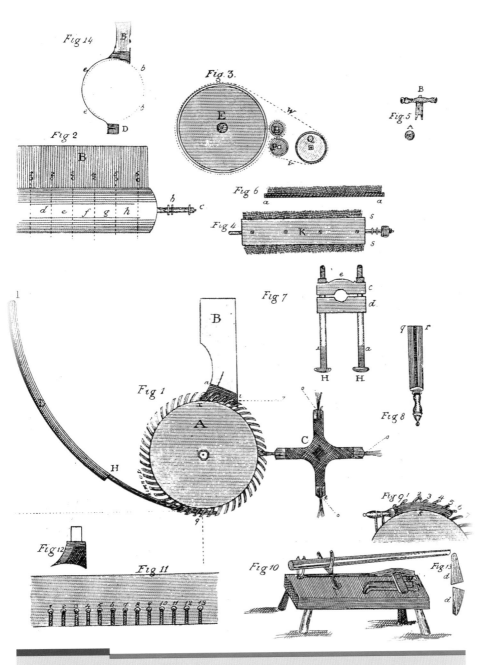

These drawings of the cotton gin were submitted by Eli Whitney to the U.S. Patent Office. Receiving a patent meant that no one except Whitney could profit from his design of the cotton gin for a certain number of years.

very simplicity of his machine proved troublesome. Any mechanically minded person could look at the cotton gin and recreate it by memory. Whitney applied for patents, but illegal copies of the cotton gin soon appeared despite patent laws.

Sadly, the cotton gin prolonged the institution of slavery. Shortly after the War of Independence, slavery disappeared in the northern states. It remained in the South where people often called it the "peculiar institution." Even in the South slavery was beginning to fade because it simply was not profitable for farmers to keep slaves. Then, suddenly, Whitney's invention made cotton king in the southern states. Cotton crops jumped from 85 million pounds in 1810 to 160 million in 1820.[8] Cotton farmers enjoyed the large profits and became dependent on slavery. King Cotton meant slavery became a moneymaker once more.

The issue of slavery divided the nation into separate and hostile camps. Several southern states seceded (declared themselves separate) from the union. Then, on April 12, 1861, southern forces fired on Fort Sumter in the harbor of Charleston, South Carolina. The American Civil War began. The war lasted four years and took more lives than any other conflict in U.S. history.

The Industrial Revolution and the great divide between the South and the North played a part in the war's final outcome. The industrialized North had twice as many miles of railroad track as did the South. Northern factories churned out more rifles than did

The Monitor Battles the Merrimac

One Civil War battle changed naval warfare forever. On March 9, 1862, the southern ship C.S.S. *Merrimac* (also called the *Virginia*) met the northern vessel U.S.S. *Monitor* in the waters off Hampton Roads, Virginia. Both were ironclads, meaning their sides were covered with iron plating. Both were powered by steam engines. For four hours, the two ironclads bombarded each other with their cannons. On several occasions, they came so close that their hulls actually touched. Crew members working inside the iron giants suffered in oven-like heat. Yet, amazingly, no one was killed. Cannon shells simply bounced off the sides of the two vessels. Steam power and iron plating, both products of the Industrial Revolution, were combined to produce these two ships. Other nations studied this sea battle as a naval turning point. For hundreds of years sea warfare was waged by wooden ships propelled by sails. After this four-hour battle, the age of wooden warships ended and the modern battleship emerged.

The battle between the *Monitor* and the *Merrimac* signaled the end of wooden, sail-powered ships and the beginning of iron, steam-driven vessels.

manufacturers in the South. Factories generate money. Consequently, banks in the northern states held far more cash than their southern counterparts.

The Civil War ended on April 9, 1865, in a triumph for the northern forces. Slavery was abolished and the American Union restored. The war left the defeated South in ruins while the North enjoyed prosperity based on its industrial might. In the years after the Civil War, iron, steam power, and ingenious machines altered American life to a degree no one had dreamed possible.

The
Transformation
of Life and Work

Farm machinery now gives the farmer an amount of leisure unknown in the old times of hand labor. All the really hard work is done by machines. We cannot suppose this to be detrimental to the intellect and character of the farm population. Leisure is the golden dream of the working classes all over the world, and if the modern farmer has secured release in part from the grinding toil that made of his father an old man at fifty . . . who shall say that he has been injured thereby in brain force or moral stamina?[1]

E.V. Smalley, from an article called "Has Farm Machinery Destroyed Farm Life?" which appeared in *The Forum* magazine in April 1894.

Consider the day-to-day life of a man or a woman born in the United States in the 1840s. He or she would probably live on a farm. The American of the time would read a book at night by candlelight, sew clothes by hand, and rarely venture more than a few miles from home. That person, born in the infancy of the American Industrial Revolution, lived to see miracles. By the time he or she reached old age, electric lights glowed in American homes. Sewing machines made and repaired clothes. In a span of just one long lifetime, typewriters, telephones, cross-country trains, and even flying machines appeared.

All these new products were brought into use as a result of the Industrial Revolution. This powerful movement in history changed life so fast that it separated the generations. Many people born in 1900 could not imagine a world without the electric light. That was the past era, the darker world of their fathers and mothers.

This sewing machine was the first one designed by Isaac Singer, in 1853. He first named it the "Jenny Lind" after a famous Swedish singer at that time.

Electric lighting came about through the genius of Thomas Alva Edison (1847–1931). Born in Milan, Ohio, Edison grew up driven by a burning need to learn. His mother was a schoolteacher. As a boy Thomas constantly fired questions at her. Some of the questions were difficult for her to come up with a simple explanation: "What makes water put out a fire?"

Edison attended school

for only a few months. Studying lessons in a classroom was too slow a process for him. Instead, he learned by self-study and experimentation. As a young man, he developed a special telegraph (called a stock ticker) that transmitted gold prices. With the profits he received from the stock ticker, he opened a laboratory in Menlo Park, New Jersey. Working from the lab, Edison devoted his life to invention. He invented the first successful phonograph and motion picture machine. So many incredible devices came from his New Jersey laboratory that Thomas Edison earned the nickname "The Wizard of Menlo Park."

Edison's electric light dramatically changed life for millions of people around the world. A large apparatus called an arc light already existed. Arc lights produced a glow by generating an electrical spark. Edison hoped to create a small electric light for use in homes and offices. He knew electricity passing through a thin wire (a filament) would cause the wire to cast a light. But the wire quickly burned out. Edison tried dozens of different materials in his search for a long-lasting filament. He once used red hair plucked from the beard of a friend. In 1879, he passed electricity through a sewing thread which had been burned to an ash. He covered the thread with a bulb to keep out oxygen, which would hasten burning. The combination of a new filament material protected by a bulb produced a bright light which lasted many hours. Edison had created the lightbulb. In effect, the Wizard of Menlo Park succeeded in turning night into day.

Alexander Graham Bell (1847–1922) was born in Scotland. His father specialized in teaching deaf children how to speak properly. Young Alexander also became a teacher of the deaf. He grew particularly interested in how sound travels. After moving to the United States, in 1872 Alexander opened a special school to train teachers of deaf children in Boston. He also studied the telegraph. He wondered if the electrical telegraph could be made to carry the sounds of the human voice instead of the simple dots and dashes.

Bell worked with a friend, Thomas Watson, who understood electricity. Their early attempts to transmit words through wires failed. One day in 1876, Bell accidentally spilled battery acid on his clothes. Without thinking he said into his experimental telephone device, "Mr. Watson, come here. I want you!" Watson, who was in a different room, heard the voice through the wires. Thus the telephone was born.

The amazing devices of the Industrial Revolution came to the American public not just as novel curiosities, but as everyday items to be used by the masses. Factories turned out the new products at incredible rates. An item such as a lightbulb, which in 1840 would be thought of as a magical thing, became both common and affordable in an astonishingly short period of time. In 1890 alone, more than one million lightbulbs were sold, even though the product was just eleven years old. Just twenty-five years after Bell's

This is one of the early versions of Alexander Graham Bell's telephone.

telephone was invented, some 1.3 million phones were in use in the nation.

Industry Begets Industry

Railroads made spectacular advances in the post-Civil War years. By 1900, five transcontinental railroads were in operation, and the United States had far more miles of track than did all of Europe.

Innovations within the railroad business created many sub-industries. In the 1890s, the Swift Company of Chicago pioneered the use of refrigerator cars to carry fresh meat to eastern cities. Factories were set up which produced nothing but refrigerator cars. Also in Chicago, the Pullman Company made marvelous

Wired President

Benjamin Harrison, who served as the president of the United States from 1889 to 1893, brought electric lighting to the White House. However, electricity inside homes was such a new concept that President and Mrs. Harrison refused to turn the lights on or off. They feared receiving a deadly shock from the switches. Servants operated the White House lights for them.

sleeper cars which allowed passengers to sleep in a real bed while taking long train trips. George Westinghouse (1846–1914) invented an air-brake that safely stopped trains and prevented accidents. Plants in Pittsburgh produced the Westinghouse airbrake and other devices which benefited the railroads.

The American Industrial Revolution depended on the steel industry. Steel is an alloy, or mixture, of iron, carbon, and other materials. It is lighter than iron and just as strong. For years, builders and machine-makers shunned steel because it was too expensive. Then, a British metallurgist named Henry Bessemer (1813–1898) found a way to make steel more cheaply. The new method revolutionized the industry. Using the new Bessemer process, the United States soon made more steel than industrial plants in Great Britain and Germany combined. Steel built the sky-scrapers rising in Chicago and New York. The great steel wonder of the age, the Brooklyn Bridge, was completed in 1883 and is still in use.

Capital (money) was needed to build factories. Banks supplied the capital to businessmen. Therefore, banks became more and more powerful as the Industrial Revolution took hold. Factories required

Cannonballs and Legends

Americans in the 1890s were awed by the power and speed of locomotives. Trains regularly roared down the track at lightning speeds, 60 miles per hour and even faster. Especially speedy trains were called cannonballs. The swift trains were named for their runs—the Wabash Cannonball, the New Orleans Cannonball, and so on. Their drivers (engineers) became legends. One such engineer was John Luther "Casey" Jones, who was born in Kentucky in 1864. Jones teamed up with a highly skilled "fireman," an African American named Sim Webb. Jones worked the controls while Webb shoveled coal into the boiler keeping the fire burning. The Jones and Webb team raced their cannonball between cities delivering goods and passengers.

On the dark night of April 29, 1900, Jones and Webb drove *Engine 382*, a speedy mail train, toward New Orleans. At the last moment Jones saw a parked freight train standing on the track ahead. He shouted to Webb to jump and then applied the brake. Too late. Jones died the death of a railroad engineer with one hand on the throttle and the other on the brake. Sim Webb lived a long life and loved to tell tales of Casey Jones and his train. A famous folksong celebrated Casey Jones:

> Come all you rounders, for I want you to hear,
> The story of a brave engineer.
> Casey Jones was the rounder's name,
> On a big eight wheeler of a mighty fame.[2]

steel. Steelmaking required products from the mines such as coal and coke. Railroads shipped coal and coke as well as finished steel. One industry fed off another and American factory production soared.

In 1876, the nation held the Centennial Exposition in Philadelphia. The fairgrounds spread over 450 acres of Philadelphia's Fairmont Park. Millions of visitors

The sleeping quarters were at the back on the left side of the first Pullman sleeper car.

came to the park during the exposition's six-month run. The great fair was supposed to celebrate the hundredth anniversary of American independence. Each of the then thirty-eight states had a display. Often these displays were homegrown items—corn from Iowa and cheese from Wisconsin. But most visitors were thrilled by the fair's medley of machinery. Standing taller than a four-story house was the Corliss steam engine, the most powerful machine ever built. Some eight thousand other machines were also presented. They included sewing machines, elevators, printing presses, adding machines, and soda fountains for making ice cream creations. Also there was Alexander Graham Bell's first telephone. One foreign guest, Emperor Dom Pedro of Brazil, tried the telephone. In surprise, he exclaimed, "My God! It talks!"[3]

Change Comes to Farms

Generations of American farmers harvested wheat in the traditional manner. They cut the stalks of wheat with sickles and then tied them together by hand into bundles. It was backbreaking work performed under a hot sun. A simple wheat harvest required many field hands. Then came the

Visiting the Centennial Exposition Today

After the Philadelphia Centennial Exposition closed, much of the machinery displayed there was moved to Washington, D.C. In the nation's capital, the onetime Centennial exhibits were housed inside the Arts and Industries Building. This was the second building constructed as part of the Smithsonian Institution. The machinery can be seen to this day at the Smithsonian.

reaper, manufactured by Cyrus McCormick of Chicago. This horse-drawn machine cut the grain neatly and efficiently. By the 1890s, McCormick's reaper was replaced by the binder. The new binder cut the wheat and automatically made bundles of the wheat stalks. Using the binder, farmers harvested wheat ten times faster than they could with old hand methods.

The invention of barbed wire aided the development of western farms. Most farms in the West raised cattle as well as crops. Cattle enjoy roaming while they graze. The animals will eat any plants on the ground. Desperately needed were cheap, easy-to-install fences to keep cows away from cultivated fields. It was long known that cattle avoided plants with thorns. So, why not put steel thorns on steel wire and thereby create fences? Barbed wire was devised in the 1870s by Joseph F. Glidden (1813–1906) of DeKalb, Illinois. The thorny wire helped to transform the West. Barbed wire was a relatively simple idea. Yet the wire could not be produced in quantity without the steelmaking methods developed during the Industrial Revolution.

Although barbed wire is often used today to keep people out of private property, it was originally designed to keep cattle from wandering off their owner's land. Today, barbed wire is still used to keep a farmer's herd in one place.

The southern states were also revived due to improvements in agriculture. With the aid of new farm machinery, the South produced far more cotton than it did in the days of slavery. This boom in cotton production came despite pre-Civil War warnings by southern landowners that their plantations would go bankrupt without slave labor. Harvesting machines also allowed the South to double its tobacco production. Sugar farming in the south improved due to new machinery too.

Mechanization, however, was a mixed blessing on American farms. What the Industrial Revolution gave to farmers with one hand, it often took away with the other. Few farmers had enough ready cash to buy a machine such as McCormick's reaper. So a farmer had to borrow money to buy the harvesting device. After borrowing the money from a bank, the farmer hoped his fall harvest would earn enough to pay off the debt. Harvests were easily ruined by drought, flood, grasshopper infestations, or other disasters. A bad harvest spelled doom for a debt-ridden farmer. Banks often took over the farmer's land because of unpaid loans.

The farmer was also hampered by middlemen. The middleman is a financial institution which grew with the Industrial Revolution. Middlemen owned milling companies and meatpacking plants. They bought raw crops from farmers, processed them, and sold them to consumers. One such middleman was Charles Alfred Pillsbury (1842–1899). Pillsbury established a small flour mill in Minnesota in 1869. Using the latest milling machinery, C.A. Pillsbury & Company became

Booker T. Washington, Voice of the New South

African Americans comprised one-third of the post-Civil War South's population. Most were ex-slaves who lived in deep poverty in the rural areas. One African-American leader, Booker T. Washington (1856–1915), envisioned a new South. He saw a future southern economy that would combine agriculture and light industry. He hoped this new economy would improve the lives of both blacks and impoverished whites.

Born a slave, Washington founded a school in Alabama called the Tuskegee Institute. The school taught young blacks carpentry, agriculture, and other job-related skills. Washington became the advisor of presidents. Many Americans accepted him as the national spokesman for blacks. Critics, including some African Americans, claimed that Washington was fearful of offending whites and he too easily accepted racial segregation in the South. Despite the criticism, Booker T. Washington remained a powerful leader all his life.

the largest flour miller in the world. Meanwhile, the company paid the farmer the lowest possible prices for wheat. Bitterness over middleman policies led to a song, "The Farmer is the Man," which was often sung in the 1890s:

> *The farmer is the man,*
> *The farmer is the man,*
> *Lives on credit till the fall;*
> *Then they lead him by the hand*
> *And they lead him from the land—*
> *The middleman's the one who gets it all.[4]*

Railroads held farmers captive with the high rates they charged for shipping produce to market. Farmers turned to government leaders for protection from the railroads. Freight rates became one of the most hotly debated political issues in the nation. As early as the 1870s, farm states such as Minnesota, Iowa, and Wisconsin passed laws regulating freight rates and making them more affordable for the farmer. In 1887, the federal government finally acted by creating the Interstate Commerce Commission. The commission had the power to take railroads to court if they charged unfair fees. Despite the laws, railroads thrived on their fees while thousands of farmers went broke.

Pressures brought about by middlemen and railroads drove many small farmers off the land. Before the Civil War, the United States was overwhelmingly an agricultural nation. By 1900, about two-thirds of the country's workforce was engaged in nonfarm occupations. Even though the United States had far more mouths to feed and fewer farmers to work the land, the country never faced a serious food shortage. Farming was now mechanized and food production increased dramatically.

Growth of the Cities

As was true in Great Britain, American cities experienced tremendous growth due to the Industrial Revolution. Millions of people left the farms and flocked to the cities to take factory jobs. New York City, Chicago, and San Francisco saw huge population increases in the last half of the nineteenth century. The sudden growth of the cities alarmed many Americans. In 1895 the social critic Henry J. Fletcher called the movement from farms to cities, "an evil of great magnitude. It lowers the tone of village and farm life. . . . In America, even the poorest of the working people refuse to go into the country to live."[5]

Immigrants, mostly from Europe, made their homes in the cities. The newcomers earned little and had to take whatever housing they could afford. Soon, every large city included poor immigrant areas. Neighborhood streets became a babble of languages and a medley of exotic food smells. New York's lower Manhattan district was an open-air marketplace where people bought goods from pushcarts as well as from stores. Chicago had sprawling immigrant neighborhoods where foreign languages were heard more often than English.

Chicago incorporated as a town in 1833. At the time, it was a muddy little settlement on Lake Michigan with about two hundred people. By 1900, Chicago was the second-largest city in the United States. Chicago, more than most cities, was a child of the Industrial Revolution. It was both a railroad center and a factory complex. The McCormick reaper plant, the Pullman Palace Car Company, and the Armour and Swift meatpacking companies were all located in Chicago.

Typical of the industrial cities at the time, Chicago had miserable slums. Workers lived in tiny wooden cottages. Some of those cottages were hammered together in less than a week. Many city residents were foreign-born. Uneducated and unskilled, the immigrants took

In Europe and the United States the Industrial Revolution drew people to the cities. England and Germany had a majority urban population in the 1800s. The United States, with its vast lands, remained a mostly rural country until the 1920s. Here is a decade-by-decade look at America's urban expansion:

	Total Population	Urban	Rural
1860	31,443,321	19.8%	80.2%
1870	38,558,371	25.4%	74.3%
1880	50,189,209	28.2%	71.8%
1890	62,979,766	35.1%	64.9%
1900	76,212,168	39.6%	60.4%
1910	92,228,496	45.6%	54.4%
1920	106,021,537	51.2%	48.8%[6]

Note: The trend to live in cities continues to this day. The 2000 census reported the American population as 281,421,906, with 81 percent living in cities and 19 percent living in rural areas.

whatever jobs they could find and accepted whatever pay scales the bosses offered. One of the most notorious slums was the Back of the Yards neighborhood. This district sprawled near the stockyards, where animals were slaughtered and meat was processed. On windless days, the smell of the stockyards traveled more than a mile. The Back of the Yards was full of flies and had an inadequate sewage system. A lawyer for the meatpacking companies inspected the Back of the Yards and proclaimed, "You should tear down the district, burn all the houses."[7]

Children were often neglected or even abandoned by their parents in the teeming slums of Industrial Revolution cities. A children's aid society found one small boy on the New York streets with a note pinned to his shirt: "Take care of Johnny, for God's sake. I cannot."[8] Young men turned to crime as they watched their parents struggle through life burdened by low factory wages. An 1899 study of conditions in Boston reported that "Almost every boy in the [South End slums] is member of a gang. The boy who does not belong to one is not only the exception but the very rare exception."[9]

Labor Transformed

The use of interchangeable parts, introduced by Eli Whitney, was a key to the manufacturing miracles achieved during the Industrial Revolution. Machines turned out parts far faster than human hands could produce them. Once the parts were made, humans assembled them into typewriters, adding machines, and cash registers.

But the principle of interchangeable parts also made workers interchangeable. At one time, a skilled craftsman was able to build a horse-drawn wagon from the wheels up. The Industrial Revolution and interchangeable parts rendered such skills unnecessary. The wagon maker now toiled over a machine that churned out nothing but the spokes for the wagon wheels. Other factory hands put the wagon together somewhere else down the assembly line.

Gone was the pride a worker felt from creating a finished product. Gone were the work skills learned and cherished over many years. Now women sat over sewing machines in shirt factories cutting and sewing one thousand identical buttonholes in the course of a day. Men toiled in machine shops drilling one thousand same-size holes in one thousand pieces of metal. An 1888 New York report decried this development because it denied vocational skills to youth: "Where, in former times, boys were expected to learn a trade in all its features, they are now simply put at a machine or at one branch of the craft, and no understanding exists that they shall be taught any other branch or the use of any other machine."[10]

Relegating factory hands to produce only parts of a whole came to be called "piecework." This was a proper description. Workers simply made pieces of something larger. Piecework led to another Industrial Revolution practice called the "sweating system" and to the growth of "sweatshops." In a sweatshop people crowded together in airless apartments in the summer heat. Despite the heat, the people worked furiously to produce their pieces. Naturally the workers sweated profusely under these conditions. Often a worker in a sweatshop was paid only by the number of pieces he or she produced in the course of a day.

The garment industry was the largest abuser of the sweating system. Immigrant apartments became sweatshops as whole families sat inside churning out pieces of cloth for the garment makers. An 1893 report written about Illinois sweatshops said that "In this country the whole ready-made clothing trade rests upon the sweating system in some of its various forms."[11]

At one time, a man's suit or a woman's dress was tailor-made by a single craftsperson. Then came the Industrial Revolution with its emphasis on cheap, mass-produced goods. By the close of the nineteenth century, garments were ready-made and assembly-line produced. Suits and dresses dropped in price, but wages for the people making the garments were low. Often a woman working on a sewing machine in a sweatshop could not afford the dresses she was helping to make.

Child labor was another evil associated with the American Industrial Revolution. Boys as young as twelve toiled as "breaker boys," picking rocks out of heaps of coal. Girls worked on milling machines in textile factories. Sometimes a mill girl put in a sixteen-hour work shift. Working long hours meant a child had little time for school or for play.

In 1900, a writer named John Spargo visited a bottling plant in the South. The factory produced cheap bottles. It employed dozens of breaker boys to process coal before the coal went to the furnaces. Spargo described the scene:

> Work in the coal breakers is exceedingly hard and dangerous. Crouched over the chutes, the boys sit hour after hour, picking out pieces of slate and other refuse from the coal as it rushes past to the washers. From the cramped position they have to

Child labor was often used to remove rocks from the coal that powered locomotives and other steam engines. Called "breaker boys," these children were exposed to dirty and unhealthy conditions and hard labor.

assume most of them become more or less deformed and bent-backed like old men. . . . The coal is hard and accidents to the hands such as cut, broken or crushed fingers, are common among the boys. Sometimes there is a worse accident; a terrified shriek is heard, and a boy is mangled and torn in the machinery or disappears in the chute to be picked out later, smothered and dead.[12]

Women in the Workplace

Even before the Industrial Revolution, the work of a farmwoman was hard. It took an entire day to do a week's worth of family washing. The woman's hands became rough and blistered from scrubbing and wringing wet clothes. Long after other family members were asleep, women sat by candlelight sewing and mending. Also, the life of a farmwoman was limited. Traditionally a young farmgirl received fewer years of schooling than did her brothers. She was expected to marry young, raise children, and cook and wash for her family.

As the Industrial Revolution altered America, it radically changed life for working-class women. New jobs created by industry allowed women to leave their parents' homes without having to get married. This freedom alone was life-changing. But again, the Industrial Revolution had a way of taking as it gave. Women found independence and new ways to make a living. They also found drudgery in the factory and near-starvation wages in the garment industry.

Early in the Industrial Revolution, cotton-mill owners learned that women were more dexterous than men. Their hands were nimbler and able to do fine work with delicate material. So women were put to work tending machines which produced threads. Under female hands the threads rarely broke.

Mill towns were home to thousands of young women. The most celebrated of these mill towns was Lowell, Massachusetts. "Lowell girls" lived in boarding houses and worked at the town's milling companies. Civic leaders in Lowell took pride in creating a wholesome atmosphere for the young ladies. They encouraged education and sponsored events such as evening dances.

One Lowell girl was Marie Stevens. She joined a Lowell mill company in 1850 at the age of fourteen. Marie needed a job to support her two younger sisters after their mother's death. By age twenty-one, Marie had risen to the rank of supervisor. She also educated herself by studying at night in the town's library. She later became a schoolteacher. Marie Stevens worked at a time when the mills of Lowell were a positive example of industrialization enhancing people's lives. As the years passed, however, even the Lowell factories began to take advantage women workers.

The cigarmaking business also relied upon women. Cigarmaking was often conducted in cramped New York City apartments. One witness reported to a New York labor commission, "I see women surrounded by filth with children waddling in it, and having sores on

Lowell, Massachusetts Today

A leading factory in Lowell was the Boott Cotton Mill, established in 1835. For seventy-five years, the Boott millyard provided employment for women. The factory was powered by waterwheels on Lowell's canal system. Today, major buildings have been preserved at the Boott Mill Cotton Mills Museum in Lowell. Visitors are welcome to this factory complex. In its prime, it was called a "Cathedral of Industry."

their hands and faces and various parts of the body . . . They are all the time handling this tobacco they make into cigars."[13]

Women were reluctant to join labor unions. It was difficult for them to quit one job and seek another because many factories refused to hire women workers. Some industries singled out women to do the dirtiest and lowest-paying jobs on the market.

Unscrupulous employers knew impoverished women were desperate to take any job. A New Jersey labor commission wrote, "Women and child labor is much lower priced than that of men . . . the hours of labor are longer and the rate of wages less, women never agitate, they merely 'toil and scrimp, and bear.'"[14]

Tycoons and Toilers

"Not evil, but good, has come to the [human] race from the accumulation of wealth by those who have the ability and energy that produce it."[1]

The industrialist and multi-millionaire Andrew Carnegie (1835–1919).

"Poverty deepens as wealth increases, and wages are forced down . . ."[2]

Henry George (1839–1897), a social reformer and critic of America's industrial society.

Rich, Poor, and Middle Class

In the thirty-five years after the Civil War, the United States rose from being the world's fourth-largest industrial nation to the first. By 1900, America's industrial output was greater than that of England, Germany, and

France combined. In the same thirty-five-year period, the nation's population more than doubled. Immigrants poured into the country at the rate of almost a half million a year. Cities swelled as both farmers and immigrants moved into urban areas seeking factory jobs.

The Industrial Revolution produced great wealth for the few. By 1900, hundreds of Americans had become millionaires. A handful of extremely wealthy people counted their fortune in the hundreds of millions. Wealthy families lived in mansions staffed by servants. New York City's Fifth Avenue was called Mansion Row because of all the rich people's houses there. Prairie Avenue in Chicago was home to that city's richest families. The overall nature of wealth had shifted. Early in the nation's history, wealth was measured by land ownership. During the Industrial Revolution, rich people lived in cities and made their money in manufacturing. The richest manufacturing owners were called tycoons.

The middle class grew and enjoyed a comfortable life style. Middle-class people included small business owners and professionals such as doctors and lawyers. Families of the middle class could afford fascinating new devices such as the camera and the phonograph. In the early 1900s, a few middle-class people bought the latest symbol of prosperity—the automobile.

On the bottom of American society were the poor. Unskilled factory workers toiled sixty-hour workweeks. They lived in teeming slums, and barely earned enough to feed their families. Workers enjoyed no job security. A factory hand could show up one morning and discover that his or her job had been eliminated by a new machine the boss just purchased. Also, the factory workers suffered in business slowdowns such as

"God gave me my money."
—John D. Rockefeller, oil tycoon.

those that occurred in 1884 and 1893. During those slowdowns entire factories often shut their doors. Thousands of workers lost their jobs.

The huge gap between wealthy Americans and the impoverished masses almost led to a new civil war erupting in the country. The late 1800s and early 1900s were a time of bitter labor strikes and class hatred. The government, which in a democracy was supposed to represent all the people, too often favored the rich.

The Captains of Industry

The Industrial Revolution helped to make John D. Rockefeller (1839–1937) the richest person on earth. He once said, "God gave me my money."[3] This was the same attitude that Old World kings and queens once held. The monarchs believed it was God's wish that they should live above the masses and enjoy comforts undreamed of by commoners. But by no account was Rockefeller a greedy and self-serving man. During his lifetime he gave millions of dollars to charitable organizations. He was an American captain of industry and a complex individual.

Born in New York State, Rockefeller moved to Cleveland with his family when he was fourteen. His father worked as a peddler, buying and selling goods. At age twenty-three, Rockefeller entered the oil business. Fifteen years later, he formed the Standard Oil Company which grew to be America's most powerful business organization. Rockefeller was ruthless when dealing with competitors. He paid Standard Oil workers a bare minimum wage. He fired "troublemakers" who urged other workers to form a union. Yet he gave generously. In 1890 he donated millions of dollars to help found the University of Chicago. Today, the University of Chicago is one of the nation's most respected colleges. In 1913, the oil tycoon established the Rockefeller Foundation which sponsors programs designed to combat hunger and disease throughout the world.

Another captain of industry was Andrew Carnegie (1835–1919). Born in Scotland, his family was a victim of the Industrial Revolution. Carnegie's father worked as a weaver in the town of Dunfermline, Scotland. The introduction of steam machinery destroyed the father's livelihood. The Carnegie family immigrated

Family of Achievers

Long after John D. Rockefeller died, his family members continued to make an impact on American society. In 1946, John David Rockefeller Jr., his only son, donated money to buy eighteen acres of prime land in New York City for the United Nations headquarters building. Nelson Rockefeller (1908–1979), his grandson, served as Vice President of the United States from 1974 to 1977. Nelson Rockefeller was also Governor of New York, and he was a serious candidate for the presidency during the 1960s.

to the United States when Andrew was thirteen. Andrew worked in a cotton mill near Pittsburgh, Pennsylvania.

Always ambitious, Andrew Carnegie sensed that iron and steel were transforming the world economy. As a young man, he established a steel plant in Homestead, Pennsylvania. The plant used the new Bessemer method to process steel. Andrew Carnegie rose to become one of the richest men in the world. His company eventually developed into the giant U.S. Steel Corporation.

As was true with Rockefeller, Carnegie was selfish toward employees but generous to his nation. The 1892 Homestead Strike at his steel plant was put down by armed guards who killed several workers. Yet Carnegie gave millions to establish public libraries and schools.

After he retired, Andrew Carnegie published several books including *The Empire of Business* (1902), *Problems of Today* (1908), and his autobiography.

Many American small towns owe the start of their library systems to grants from Andrew Carnegie. Philanthropy (the giving of money to worthy causes) was almost a religion to him. He believed the accumulation of money was a man's God-given right. He also believed that to die rich was almost sinful. He wrote in 1889:

Poor and restricted are our opportunities in this life; narrow our horizons; our best work most imperfect; but rich men should be thankful for one inestimable boon. They have it in their power during their lives to busy themselves in organizing benefactions from which the masses of their fellows will derive lasting advantage, and thus dignify their own lives.[4]

Capital was the great engine that drove the Industrial Revolution. An individual or an institution with ready cash could lend money to a budding captain of industry. In that manner the entrepreneur (the hopeful factory owner) could buy machinery and build a plant. Banks and moneylenders rose in importance. The most successful of the bankers was John Pierpont Morgan (1837–1913).

Born in Hartford, Connecticut, to a well-to-do family, John Pierpont Morgan was one of the great financiers in American history. His banks lent money and helped organize giant firms such as U.S. Steel, International Harvester, General Electric, and American Telephone and Telegraph. Morgan was an intensely private man and he was generally distrusted by the American public. He was accused of heading a money trust which allowed him to secretly run the biggest businesses in the United States. Despite what was perceived to be a dark nature, he too was a generous philanthropist. A great art lover, he accumulated a magnificent collection of paintings and sculptures. Those works of art went to the New

J. P. Morgan was a very private man. Here, he strikes at a photographer with his cane.

York Metropolitan Museum of Art at his death. Morgan also gave millions to the Harvard Medical School and he founded the Lying-in Hospital in New York City.

Reformers and Progressives

Opposing the captains of industry were the champions of the working class. They included writers, labor leaders, and social reformers, who dreamed of building a better life for people in the factories and mills.

Many writers of the late 1800s and early 1900s thought it their duty to alert the middle class to the hardships suffered by the lower classes. Such writers were called muckrakers because they dug up dirt on current issues. This term came from a character in John Bunyan's book *Pilgrim's Progress*: "... a man that could look no way but downwards, with a muck-rake in his hand."[5]

Ida M. Tarbell (1857–1944) was a muckraker who attacked corruption in business in her book *History of the Standard Oil Company* (1904). Lincoln Steffens (1866–1936) wrote *Shame of the Cities* (1904) which exposed crooked politicians. Two leading muckrakers, Jacob Riis and Upton Sinclair, brought social change to the country through the power of their books.

Ida M. Tarbell's exposé of the Standard Oil Company in *McClure's* magazine and in her book helped prepare the way for reforms in the oil industry.

Jacob Riis (1849–1914) was both a writer and a photographer. In his work as a police reporter for the New York *Tribune*, he roamed the slums taking pictures of the underclass and writing about broken lives. His most famous book was *How the Other Half Lives*, published in 1890. In one section of the book he describes a Jewish immigrant slum in New York:

> Through dark hallways and filthy cellars, crowded, as is every foot of the street, with dirty children, the

settlements in the rear are reached. Thieves know how to find them when pursued by the police, and the tramps that sneak in on chilly nights to fight for the warm spot in the yard over some baker's oven. . . . Life here means the hardest kind of work almost from the cradle.[6]

Upton Sinclair (1878–1968) wrote one of the most shocking novels of his era, *The Jungle* (1906). The story followed Jurgis, a Lithuanian immigrant who worked at meatpacking plants in Chicago. Early in *The Jungle* Jurgis is given a tour of a typical plant's operations. He is overwhelmed by the pace the workers must maintain. The noise and the gore inside the slaughterhouse shock him: ". . . over the top of the pen there leaned one of the 'knockers,' armed with a sledge-hammer, and watching for a chance to deal a blow. The room echoed with thuds in quick succession, and the stamping and kicking of the steers."[7]

Jurgis notices that some of the butchers who cut meat into pieces were missing fingers. He concludes the butchers were forced to work so fast that they accidentally sliced off a finger or two while trying to keep up with the furious pace. The floor of the packinghouse is covered with blood and the entrails of animals. Jurgis hears a rumor that once a man slipped from a catwalk, fell into a vat of bubbling fat, and dissolved. His remains went to the stores, packed in cans of lard.

When writing *The Jungle*, Sinclair was moved by his early training in Christian schools and his later embrace of socialism. Upton Sinclair stood for the rights of the underdog. Many other social crusaders of the time held positive views of socialism or even Communism.

The writings of the muckrakers stirred powerful people to take action. New York City leaders read *How the Other Half Lives* and passed laws creating playgrounds and parks. *The Jungle* was read by President Theodore Roosevelt, who served in the White House from 1901 to 1908. With Roosevelt's backing, Congress passed the Pure Food and Drug Act of 1906. The act brought sanitary conditions to the meatpacking industry. Ironically, Upton Sinclair wrote *The Jungle* because he hoped the book would bring better working conditions for stockyard laborers. The very quick passage of the Pure Food and Drug Act proved that Congress and the public was more concerned about the meat they bought at stores than the plight of those who worked in the meatpacking industry.

Jane Addams (1860–1935) grew up in a large, comfortable house in the town of Cedarville, Illinois.

Jane Addams dedicated her life to helping the disadvantaged.

At the age of seven she noticed that not far from her house stood shacks where poor people lived. The children there were dirty. They wore ragged clothes, and their shoes were falling apart. Addams asked her father why their family led such a privileged life while their neighbors struggled. Her father could only shrug his shoulders. He explained that there had always been vast differences between rich and poor. Jane Addams refused to accept that explanation.

In 1889, Jane Addams moved into Hull House on the West Side of Chicago. The building was once a mansion. It was now surrounded by slum dwellings in one of the city's poorest immigrant districts. There she taught immigrant women job skills and held art classes and play readings for children. Her programs were offered free to poor people of all races. She transformed Hull House into a settlement house, a welcoming place to learn. Jane Addams' idea of philanthropy was to give of herself.

Another reformer was labor leader Eugene V. Debs (1855–1926). Born in Terre Haute, Indiana, Debs had a happy but confused childhood. His father, who worked as a laborer, urged his son to read books and study art. His mother, who ran a tiny grocery store, told Eugene to concentrate on getting a good job. Family financial problems finally decided his future. At age fourteen, Eugene Debs was forced to quit school and work. His first job was at the railroad yards. He scraped paint off old railroad cars for fifty cents a day.

He was soon promoted to be a fireman on train engines. As a fireman he got a raise to a dollar a day.

Debs read and studied as he worked for the railroads. His favorite book was *Les Misérables* by the French author Victor Hugo. The book told of a poor man who stole a loaf of bread to feed his family. The impoverished man had to serve nineteen years in prison for the theft. Debs saw similar injustices committed on the poor people of his town in Indiana. He concluded that working men and women must fight the evils of the system by forming labor unions. An excellent public speaker, Debs organized the American Railway Union (ARU) in 1893. This new union embraced all railroad employees, skilled engineers as well as common laborers. The ARU launched Eugene Debs to a prominent position in industrial America. He became not only a powerful labor leader, but the conscience of his country.

Labor Wars

The late 1800s were a violent period in American history. Labor unions regularly clashed with management in a series of bloody strikes. Labor unrest was so alarming that many Americans feared the outbreak of a war pitting the rich against the poor. Such class warfare was common in Europe, but previously unknown in the United States.

In 1877, railroad strikes spread across the country. The strikes erupted into riots where workers battled police. The public viewed the 1877 strikes with great

Eugene V. Debs

alarm. But even more violent upheavals lay ahead. Two labor conflicts, the Haymarket Massacre of 1886 and the Pullman Strike of 1894, struck fear in the hearts of the people. Both clashes took place in Chicago.

On May 1, 1886, labor leaders around the country called on American workers to hold a nationwide strike. The leaders demanded an eight-hour workday. At the time, men and women commonly worked exhausting ten- to twelve-hour shifts. Strikers rallying for the eight-hour day chanted as if they were at a football game:

Eight Hours for Work
Eight Hours for Recreation, Rest
Eight Hours for Sleep.[8]

May 1 passed without violence. Few workers walked off their jobs as union chiefs had urged them to do. Then, on May 3, a fight broke out between workers and security guards at Chicago's giant McCormick plant. Workers threw rocks at factory windows and someone fired a shot. Some two hundred Chicago police officers arrived and attacked the crowd, swinging their billy clubs. One worker was killed and more than a dozen were carried away with blood running from their heads.

To protest the police actions at the McCormick works, union leader August Spies called for a meeting at Chicago's Haymarket Square on the night of May 4. The German-born Spies was an anarchist, a person who rejected all laws. He and other anarchists rejected laws because they so often favored the rich. The anarchist message was born in Europe and spread to the United States through waves of immigration. Most Americans feared and hated the anarchists and their alien philosophy.

A terrible blast ripped the square. Police opened fire and the night erupted into a chaos of bullets.

A huge crowd of chanting and hollering people attended the May 4 meeting at Haymarket Square. They were closely watched by Chicago police. At first, the gathering was noisy but peaceful. A light rain fell and the meeting began to break up. Then someone threw a dynamite bomb into the ranks of police. A terrible blast ripped the square. Police opened fire and the night erupted into a chaos of bullets. Eight police officers and four spectators were killed, and dozens more wounded.[9]

Terror gripped Chicago and the United States. Newspaper accounts painted a ghastly picture of what they called the Haymarket Square Massacre. The New York *Tribune*, which had no reporter at the scene, wrote: "The mob [at Haymarket Square] appeared crazed with a frantic desire for blood."[10] Frightened citizens around the country believed the city of Chicago was now in the hands of European revolutionaries and terrorists.

Eight anarchist leaders were arrested and charged with inciting the mob to violence. After a hasty trial a judge sentenced seven of the accused to death. Four men, including August Spies, were hanged. The others were pardoned by Illinois Governor John Peter Altgeld (1847–1902) after serving seven years in prison. Altgeld believed the labor leaders had been denied a fair trial. Today Altgeld is praised for his courage, but at the time he was bitterly denounced for freeing the Haymarket anarchists.

Millions of excited people came to Chicago in 1893 to attend the World's Columbian Exposition. The fair celebrated the four-hundredth anniversary of Christopher Columbus' voyage to the New World. It also displayed the latest devices produced by the

May Day, A Festive Day for World Communism

At one time the grandest day of the year in the Communist Soviet Union was May 1, or May Day. It was a national holiday complete with parades and bands. Other Communist nations also held giant May Day festivals. Few Americans realized that the May Day celebrations in the Communist world honored the events of May 1, 1886, when Chicago workers rallied for the eight-hour day. An 1889 meeting of world socialist parties in Paris voted to make May Day a holiday in support of American workers. Today, Communism has faded in what was once the Soviet Union and the May Day celebrations have lost much of their glamour.

On display at the World Columbian Exposition were a balloon and a Ferris wheel.

Industrial Revolution. Spectators were thrilled when visiting the Electricity Building which was bathed in the glow of thousands of lightbulbs. Others screamed in delight as they rode the 250-foot Ferris wheel, the first of its kind.

Many fair visitors took a special train to tour the town of Pullman, Illinois, near the Chicago city limits. Here was a clean, neat community where nine thousand workers and their families lived in row houses. The town was the inspiration of George Pullman, the maker of railroad sleeping cars. In the middle of the town sprawled the giant Pullman factory building. Working men and women lived in the houses. They paid rent to the Pullman Company, shopped at the Pullman Company store, and even worshipped at a church built by Pullman. Fair-goers walked the streets of this model town and hailed the genius of George Pullman, its creator.

Shortly after the World's Columbian Exposition opened, an economic depression called the Panic of 1893 froze the nation's economy. At first, such depressions affect only the rich people who own stock in companies. Then the companies start losing money and lay off workers. Soon the entire nation feels the impact. The 1893 depression was severe. Some twelve thousand businesses closed and three million men and women lost their jobs.

George Pullman kept most of his workers employed, but reduced their wages. However, he did not decrease the amount of money his employees paid for rent. Pullman workers had their rent automatically deducted from their paychecks. Reduced wages coupled with regular deductions for rent equaled devastating pay cuts for the Pullman men and women. The winter of 1893 was the coldest in years. For the working people in the model town of Pullman, Illinois, it was a period of suffering, hunger, and hatred— hatred directed at George Pullman.

In May 1894, the Pullman workers went on strike, demanding fair wages and rents. George Pullman, whose company made money despite the depression, refused to meet their demands. Finally, Eugene Debs and his newly formed American Railway Union (ARU) entered the fray. Debs announced the ARU would launch a nation-wide railroad strike in sympathy with the Pullman employees. Around the country, railroad workers walked off their jobs. It was the largest industry-wide strike in American history.

The Pullman Strike came at a desperate time. Nationwide unemployment was high due to the Panic of 1893. Many working-class Americans blamed the railroad industry for the country's economic troubles. Starving people held angry meetings at Chicago's railroad yards. Railroad owners hired a small army of gun-carrying security guards to protect their property. This already tense situation was made even more volatile by the actions of the U.S. government and Attorney General Richard Olney. Olney (1835–1917) claimed the Pullman Strike interfered with the nation's mail. Most mail at the time was delivered by rail. The attorney general secured an injunction (a court order) making the strike illegal. Strike leaders, including Eugene Debs, were now subject to arrest.

On the night of July 4, 1894, riots broke out in Chicago. Groups of workers fought with security guards and attacked freight cars in railroad yards. When they reached the cars men and women carried away cans of meat, sacks of potatoes, or whatever goods they could find. Many rioters threw blazing torches into railroad buildings. One observer wrote, "I saw huge mobs running wild [. . .] putting the torch to

RECEIVING AND QUESTIONING APPLICANTS FOR APPOINTMENTS AS DEPUTIES
AT THE MARSHAL'S OFFICE, CHICAGO.

CHICAGO AND NORTHWESTERN RAILROAD ROUND-HOUSE, JULY 3, 1894—No.1
AN ENGINE MOVING.

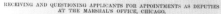

These drawings show the impact that the Pullman Strike had on Chicago. This impact was also felt throughout the country.

millions of dollars' worth of property[. . . .] Could such anarchy be permitted in a civilized society?"[11]

The rioting continued through the first week in July. President Grover Cleveland sent federal troops to Chicago and finally order was restored. During a week of fighting, scores of people were killed or injured and property damage cost millions of dollars. The Pullman Strike of 1894 was viewed as more than just another labor dispute. In the minds of the people it was a war between rich and poor.

Most important was the role played by the government in the Pullman conflict. The injunction issued by a federal court made the strike illegal. To the strikers, this meant the U.S. government sided with the railroad companies. The injunction added fuel to arguments advanced by the anarchists that government will always represent the rich, never the workers. This belief in a probusiness American government further frustrated the working class.

The Pullman Strike did produce a working-class hero in Eugene Debs. The 1894 disorder in Chicago thrust Debs into the public eye, where he remained the rest of his life. Debs went to prison for six months for his role in the Pullman Strike. It would not be his last time behind bars. He ran for president five times as a candidate for the Socialist Party. In 1918, he spoke against American involvement in World War I. He was jailed under a measure called the Espionage Law, which punished people for criticizing the war effort. Despite being in prison, Debs received more than one million votes for president in the 1920 election.

Eugene Debs was loved by poor people who believed he was one of them. His views on the working class are seen in the words of a poem he wrote while in jail. The poem is called "My Prison Creed."

> *While there is a lower class I am in it;*
> *While there is a criminal element I am of it;*
> *While there is a soul in prison I am not free.*[12]

The Industrial Revolution in the Twentieth Century

Now, my plan is to have organized union labor Americanized in the best sense and thoroughly educated to an understanding of its responsibilities, and in this way to make it the ally of the capitalist, rather than a foe.[1]

Mark Hanna, writing in 1904. Hanna (1837–1904) made millions in the iron business and was elected a U.S. senator from Ohio. Though he was a corporation owner, Hanna believed big business must cooperate with labor unions and bring peace to industrialized America.

The Progressive Era

By the turn of the twentieth century, Americans counted the blessings brought to them by industrialization. Trains took passengers to just about every city in the country. Electric lighting was in use in cities, though it had not yet come to the farms. Many houses and offices were served by telephones.

Despite the wonders of the age, the public could not forget the labor wars of the late 1800s. The Industrial Revolution brought miracles, but it also fostered hostilities between rich and poor. Then, in the early 1900s, tempers began to cool. The government took steps to ease the hardships of workers and reduce the power held by corporation owners. This led to what was called the Progressive Era, a time of change prompted by government reforms.

Big business was a product of the Industrial Revolution. Men such as John D. Rockefeller and Andrew Carnegie were able to buy up small companies and absorb them into their own giant firms. Such huge companies were called trusts. The owners of trusts controlled entire industries. Without competition, the trusts set prices and wages as they wished. Tycoons such as Rockefeller and Carnegie often wielded more power over the country than did the president.

In 1890, Congress passed the Sherman Antitrust Act. Language in the act made trusts illegal because they stifled competition. For the first ten years of its life, the Sherman Antitrust Act did little to discourage the formation of giant companies. Corporation owners held enormous political power and few government leaders were willing to challenge them.

In 1901, President William McKinley was shot and killed by an anarchist named Leon Czolgosz. The assassin later said he had an overwhelming desire to

The Triangle Shirtwaist Fire

Appalling conditions in some American factories were exposed in 1911 by a tragic fire. The Triangle Shirtwaist Company in New York City produced shirts and other textile goods. The company employed mostly Jewish and Italian immigrant girls and women aged thirteen to twenty-three. On March 25, 1911, just as the employees were ready to leave the building, a fire broke out on the lower floors. Fed by loose cloth, the fire soon raged out of control. Many doors to the factory were locked. Other doors opened inward and became jammed by the crush of employees wanting to escape. Some of the young women jumped nine floors to their deaths rather than die in the fire. In all, 146 people were killed in one of America's worst industrial accidents. The Triangle fire alerted Americans to unsafe conditions in factories. New laws were passed to prevent another such disaster.

Firemen race to the scene of the Triangle Shirtwaist fire. Water from the hoses on the backs of these horse-drawn fire carriages could not reach the upper floors of the factory building.

kill a powerful ruler. McKinley's murder increased fears in the minds of many Americans that the country was being taken over by anarchists and other revolutionaries.

After McKinley's death, Theodore Roosevelt (1858–1919), his vice president, took office. At age forty-two, Roosevelt was the youngest man ever to serve as president. He brought fresh ideas to the White House. He was not afraid of angering giant corporations. Roosevelt became a "trust buster," a man who forced the trusts to break up into smaller businesses. During Roosevelt's presidency the government filed antitrust lawsuits against forty-three business monopolies. Even Rockefeller's Standard Oil Company was compelled to regulate its trust practices. Roosevelt took an active role in strikes. He often sided with labor. In 1902 the president settled a coal strike by threatening to send the army to take over coal mines unless the mine owners listened to the workers' complaints.

Roosevelt's successors as president, the Republican William Howard Taft and the Democrat Woodrow Wilson, also acted to break up trusts. The Clayton Antitrust Act of 1914 gave the government even more power to regulate monopolies. Local and national leaders joined the progressive ranks. Mayor Samuel M. "Golden Rule" Jones of Toledo, Ohio, was famed for his fair dealings with labor unions. Senator Robert M. "Battling Bob" La Follette of Wisconsin sponsored many laws which favored workers and regulated businesses. Positive actions during the Progressive Era finally weakened the argument that government always sided with business interests in clashes with poor people.

Labor unions remained active during the Progressive Era. Most unions concentrated their demands on what was called "bread and butter" issues such as wages and hours. The union movement orga-

One union called upon American workers to rise up in bloody revolution.

nized mainly skilled workers. This policy left the majority of workers—the millions of unskilled laborers and factory hands—unprotected by unions.

One union called upon American workers to rise up in bloody revolution. This was the Industrial Workers of the World (IWW), founded in Chicago in 1905. The IWW's followers were called "Wobblies." Militant Wobblies saw no peaceful road to change in the factories. The IWW's manifesto declared: "There is no silver lining to the clouds of darkness and despair settling down upon the world of labor. This [current] system offers only a perpetual struggle for slight relief within wage slavery."[2]

In the Progressive Era most Americans dismissed the IWW as too extreme. Wobblies were accused of being lazy and more interested in getting soft jobs than in reforming the labor movement. Fellow workers sometimes joked that the initials IWW should stand for "I Won't Work."

The Industrial Workers of the World (IWW) split into two groups in 1908 and lost much of its appeal. Over the next dozen years it faded from the American scene. Many of the one-time Wobblies became colorful oddballs who lectured men and women on the evils of the Industrial Revolution. Always the IWW will be remembered for its spirited songs. The song "Solidarity Forever," written in 1915, was the IWW's anthem. It is sung to the tune of the "Battle Hymn of the Republic:"

> *When the Union's inspiration through the*
> *   workers blood shall run,*
> *There can be no power greater anywhere*
> *   beneath the sun.*
> *Yet what force on earth is weaker than the*
> *   feeble strength of one?*
> *For the Union makes us strong.*
> *Chorus*
> *Solidarity forever, Solidarity forever, Solidarity*
> *   forever For the Union makes us strong.*[3]

Manufacturing in Peace and War

In the late 1800s electricity came to American factories. Thus the Industrial Revolution progressed from waterpower, to steam power, and finally to electrical power. Some historians have called the transition to electrical power the Second Industrial Revolution. From new electrically driven factories came a host of products for home use.

On December 17, 1903, two brothers pushed a strange-looking craft into position on the sands of

Kitty Hawk, North Carolina. The brothers were Orville and Wilbur Wright. They owned a bicycle manufacturing company in Ohio and flew gliders in their spare time. Gliders are airplanes built to sail in the winds without engines. Both brothers dreamed of putting a lightweight motor and a propeller on a glider, thus creating a machine that could fly. At Kitty Hawk they tried their first experimental model of a flying machine. Orville served as pilot because he had won a coin toss with his brother. The engine roared and the airplane struggled off of the ground. The first flight lasted twelve seconds and covered less than half the length of a football field. But the flight was successful. The airplane was born.

In August 1914, World War I broke out in Europe. At first, European young men marched off to fight, singing patriotic songs. The young men hoped to find glory on the battlefields. European leaders believed the war would be short. But military chiefs failed to calculate the effect the Industrial Revolution would have on warfare. Two recently developed weapons, machine guns and fast-firing artillery, turned battlefields into efficient killing grounds. World War I ground down to the mud and blood of the trenches. On the western front the armies of Britain and France battled the Germans. Lines of opposing trenches stretched almost 600 miles through France and Belgium. In those muddy ditches the youth of Europe bled and died.

The United States joined World War I in April

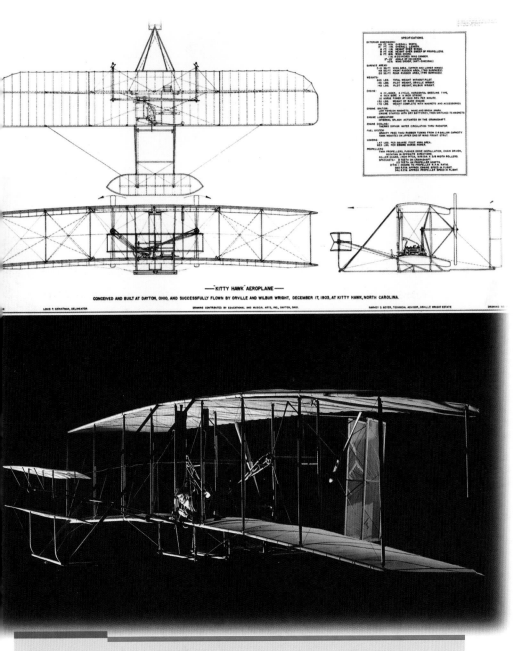

(Top) A drawing of the Wright brothers' plane. (Bottom) The Wright brothers made their first successful flight in this plane, which now hangs in the Smithsonian Institution in Washington, D.C.

1917. Allied with Great Britain and France, the fresh American troops tipped the balance of forces on the western front. Germany agreed to surrender on November 11, 1918. The war left all of Europe exhausted and depressed over the terrible loss of life. The United States in 1919 enjoyed prosperity, but it came with a price. In nineteen months of warfare, 116,516 Americans were killed and more than 320,000 were wounded.

During World War I, the demand for rifles, artillery pieces, and other tools of war stirred the economy. Factories cried out for workers. Most factories were in the northern states. This situation triggered a major population movement later called the Great Migration. The migration was headed by blacks. Prior to World War I, the vast majority of African Americans lived in the South. Many were farmers who rented their land. Often they lived in poverty, and were not much better off than in the days of slavery. As the Great Migration began thousands of southern blacks moved to the northern states.

Largely because of World War I, Communism won some important victories in Europe. The form of Communism that developed in Russia was perhaps the ultimate reaction to the Industrial Revolution. From its beginnings, the Industrial Revolution was driven by capital or investment money. In the system known as capitalism, factories and other production plants are in the hands of private investors. Under Communism, which means common or belonging to all, the people own and control the factories. In 1917, the Communists revolted and took over the war-torn nation of Russia. At the time Russia was a backward state with little industrial develop-ment. After the Communist Revolution, Russia became the Soviet Union, one of the world's lead-ing industrial powers.

In the early twentieth century, families gathered around radios much like some of today's families gather around televisions.

In the 1920s, consumer goods rolled out of American factories and new industries were born. Electricity came to millions of homes. Having electrical power allowed families to buy vacuum cleaners, washing machines, and other laborsaving devices. In 1919, only one out of three American homes had a radio. By 1929, two out of three households enjoyed radio broadcasts in their living rooms. Radio transformed life in America. Streets became strangely silent on Saturday nights. Families stayed inside and gathered around the living room radio to hear their favorite singers.

The automobile was one of America's most wildly popular innovations. In 1924, Henry Ford launched the country's car culture by dropping the price of his Model T car to $290. Ford was able to cut costs by mass-producing cars at breathtaking rates. The

At first, Henry Ford's Model T was only made in black.

reduced price allowed a skilled factory worker to buy a car. Competing automakers also cut their prices. During the decade of the 1920s the number of automobiles tripled. Most Americans wanted cars. In 1925, a reporter asked a farmwoman why her family had bought a car when they did not yet have a bathroom. The woman answered, "You can't go to town in a bathtub."[4]

The 1920s was a decade devoted to hero worship. Babe Ruth, baseball's home run king, was idolized. Movie stars such as Greta Garbo and Rudolph Valentino were larger-than-life figures. The biggest hero of the decade was Charles Lindbergh. On May 20,

1927, Lindberg boldly took his airplane across the Atlantic. Just twenty-four years earlier the Wright Brothers launched the first flight of a powered aircraft. Now this handsome young pilot climbed into his single-engine airplane on Long Island in New York and completed a thirty-three-hour solo flight to Paris, France. The country went wild cheering this bold aviator who became the first man to fly across the Atlantic alone.

The decade was called the Roaring Twenties. It was a time of zany antics such as flagpole sitting or goldfish swallowing. This period of fun and frolic was fueled by a booming economy. Factories were busy and the vast majority of Americans held steady jobs. True, the gap between rich and poor remained. The poor included farmers, African Americans, and new immigrants. But even the poor had high hopes that they too would soon be caught up in the spiraling economy.

Depression and Conflict

The good times of the 1920s rolled along on the strength of a booming stock market. At a stock market, a company sells shares or stocks of its business. People who buy the shares become part-owners of the company. If the company makes money, the shareholders can receive a cash payment in the form of a dividend. Also, the price of a share can increase. This allows the stockholder to sell shares and make a profit. In the 1920s, share prices of major corporations rose to historic highs. Stories prevailed that even barbers or shoeshine boys bought the right stock and earned a fortune in the market. Then came the dramatic reversals of late October 1929. In just two weeks, stock prices dropped sharply. Thousands of American investors lost fortunes. The boom had busted.

The Roaring Twenties gave way to the Great Depression of the 1930s. Money has a way of losing its flow during an economic depression. A person, fearing job loss, will put off making a major purchase such as an automobile. This means someone at the automobile plant loses his or her job. A snowballing effect takes over and unemployment and poverty spread. In 1932, perhaps the worst year of the Great Depression, one in four American workers were jobless. The Great Depression was the worst economic downturn in American history.

Fear and anger gripped the country in the early 1930s. The middle class feared a violent Communist revolution. Workers, desperately trying to feed their families, blamed the rich for their plight. The Industrial Revolution tied the majority of workers to factory jobs. Because of the Great Depression, entire factories closed down, leaving hungry men and women idle and upset. An investment advisor named Sidney Weinberg recalled the bitter days of the 1930s: "We were on the verge of something. You could have had rebellion; you could have had a civil war."[5]

In 1932 Americans elected Franklin Delano Roosevelt as their president. Roosevelt immediately launched a program called the New Deal. Under this program the government employed jobless men and women. The unemployed were set to work building schools or cutting hiking trails through national forests. In many respects the New Deal defied the principles of the Industrial Revolution. For more than one hundred years, the Industrial Revolution was motivated by profits. Investors built factories or textile

The Great Depression of the 1930s was a worldwide calamity which hit industrial nations the hardest.

mills hoping to gain financial rewards. There were no profits to be made in improving parklands. The New Deal concentrated on hiring those left behind by the Industrial Revolution.

Historians still argue whether or not the New Deal actually brought the country out of the Great Depression. Under New Deal measures the employment situation brightened. However, even in 1939, some 17 percent of American workers had no jobs. It took a menacing development overseas to drastically change the economy and cure unemployment.

The Great Depression of the 1930s was a worldwide calamity which hit industrial nations the hardest. Germany was still suffering from defeat in World War I when the Great Depression cost that nation millions of jobs. On some street corners, Communist speakers urged the Germans to take over their government by force. Another street-corner speaker, Adolf Hitler, drew large audiences among the Germans. Hitler preached Fascism, the opposite of Communism. Under Fascism the factories and mines stay in private hands while the government rules the lives of individuals. Hitler and the Fascists achieved power in Germany in 1933. In September 1939, Germany attacked neighboring Poland, thereby starting World War II. The United States joined World War II in December 1941, after Germany's ally Japan bombed Pearl Harbor in Hawaii.

World War II cost more lives than any conflict in human history. At its peak, more than half the world's population was caught up in the war's whirlwind.

Rosie the Riveter

With men in the armed forces, wartime industrial plants cried out for workers, and women answered the call. By the end of the war, 19 million American workers, 36 percent of the workforce, were female. Working women represented a sharp break with tradition. In the 1930s, women were expected to stay at home, cook, and tend to household chores. During the war years, the symbol of American industrial might was Rosie the Riveter. On government posters she was an attractive woman, wearing coveralls, and flexing a muscle while saying, "We can do it." Tradition says that Rosie worked in shipyards, but in fact all wartime female factory hands were "Rosies." Without the help of an army of Rosie the Riveters the United States could not have waged World War II.

Factory output during World War II proved that American industry had greatly progressed during the Industrial Revolution. This man is working on aircraft parts.

Estimates say the war took as many as 50 million lives. It was largely a war of machines. No country made more machines than did the United States. To meet wartime demands American factories produced thousands of tanks and airplanes. In a typical month in 1943, the United States manufactured more light machine guns than did Japan during the entire length of the war.

Postwar Prosperity

On August 6, 1945, a huge B-29 bomber, *Enola Gay*, roared over Japan. At 8:15 A.M. the airplane dropped a single atomic bomb on the city of Hiroshima. One airplane. One bomb. And the world has never been the same since. The bomb burst into a tremendous ball of fire, killing almost one hundred thousand people in less than a minute.

The atomic bomb was developed in a secret program called the Manhattan Project. Thousands of Americans worked on the Manhattan Project, but only a handful knew its goal. From its beginnings, the Industrial Revolution had created products for peace and weapons for war. The atomic bomb was the ultimate weapon—one that could someday destroy all life on earth.

Three days after the Hiroshima bomb, the United States dropped a second atomic bomb on the Japanese city of Nagasaki. On August 14, 1945, Japan agreed to American surrender terms. World War II was over.

Wild celebrations rocked the streets in every

The atomic bomb was the most destructive result of the Industrial Revolution. When detonated, it created a huge mushroom cloud that reached into the atmosphere. Since 1945, historians have debated whether or not the United States should have dropped the atomic bomb on Japan.

The B-29 Superfortress

The B-29 bomber, nicknamed the Superfortress, was one of World War II's mightiest aircraft. The great bomber appeared in 1943, just forty years after Orville Wright's first flight. One interesting fact indicates how quickly airplanes were developed. The Wright Brothers' initial flight at Kitty Hawk, North Carolina, covered 120 feet. The wingspan of the Superfortress is 141 feet, or 21 feet longer than the distance covered by the Wright Brothers' first flight.

American town. After almost four years, this terrible war had finally ended. But two factors dimmed the national happiness. First, the world was now in the grips of the frightful Atomic Age. Second, many Americans feared the United States would sink back into an economic depression.

The dreaded postwar depression never emerged. Instead a period of prosperity powered the economy. Through four years of war, Americans were unable to buy new cars because automobile plants concentrated on producing tanks and other military vehicles. In 1946 cars began rolling off the assembly lines again. Soon automobile traffic was so dense the government had to build better roads. In the 1950s a massive highway-building program was launched. New products appeared, and none was more popular than television. In 1945 only about ten thousand television sets operated in American homes. By 1950, the number of TVs soared to 6 million. Ten years later some 60 million television sets were in use. Americans enjoyed their consumer goods, which were the fruits of the Industrial Revolution.

The Industrial Revolution Today

The biggest mass migration in the history of the world is under way in China, and it is creating what some are calling the second industrial revolution.[1]

A news report issued by the British Broadcasting Company (BBC) on May 11, 2004.

Industrialized Asia

The Industrial Revolution continues to this day. But the process known as industrialization has shifted dramatically in recent years. No longer is the United States the manufacturing giant it once was. Today Asia leads the world in manufacturing enterprises. China produces more television sets, radios, refrigerators, textiles, and footwear than any other nation. Japan, with less than half the U.S. population, makes more automobiles than does the United States.

Does this shift to Asia mean that Americans have lost the benefits of the Industrial Revolution? Not at all. Certainly the American worker lives better than his or her Chinese counterpart. However, the Chinese standard of living is rising. China is already an industrial power.

Asia as a major manufacturing center is the latest development in the two-hundred-year-old Industrial Revolution. Computers and the Internet are other

A Japanese worker helps to build a car called the Prius in one of the Toyota Motor Corporation's many factories.

recent developments. Some historians call the Internet the Communications Revolution or the Information Age. Asia plays a major role in this newest branch of the Industrial Revolution. India is now a leading country in developing computer technology.

As was true in Europe and the United States, the Industrial Revolution sweeping Asia has caused tremendous changes in peoples' lives. Urban growth is one of those inevitable changes. For centuries, the vast majority of Chinese people lived in farming communities. China now has 22 cities with a population of more than 2 million. And this trend continues. Said Guy

Although Asia is doing well in various industries, American factories still see success. Here, a worker puts the finishing touches on a motorcycle at the Harley Davidson factory in York, Pennsylvania.

Hollis, an international real estate expert, "In the next 25 years, 345 million people [in China] are going to move from the rural areas into the city areas, which is the greatest mass migration of people ever, anywhere."[2]

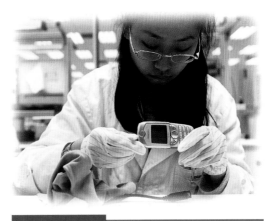

A Chinese woman works on a Siemens brand cell phone in a Shanghai factory.

By the early 1700s, The Industrial Revolution had begun in Great Britain. It spread to Europe and moved across the ocean to the United States. The revolution is now making a major impact in Asia. Wherever the Industrial Revolution advanced it erased an old way of life and created a new one. This process holds true in modern times.

1700 Most people in England live in farming communities and pursue a way of life unchanged for hundreds of years.

1707 Great Britain is created with the Act of Union which united the Kingdom of England and Wales with the Kingdom of Scotland.

1712 Thomas Newcomen of England develops an improved water pump driven by steam.

1760 Many historians regard this year as the start of the Industrial Revolution because the British textile industry began near this time.

1764 The Englishman James Hargreaves invents the spinning jenny, a textile-making device.

1769 The British engineer James Watt devises an efficient steam engine; Sir Richard Arkwright builds the water frame, a weaving machine which runs on water power.

1776 The American colonies declare themselves independent from Great Britain.

1779 Samuel Crompton builds the spinning mule, which combines features of the water frame and the spinning jenny.

1790 Samuel Slater builds a textile mill in Pawtucket, Rhode Island; it is the first large factory to operate in the United States.

1791 U.S. Secretary of the Treasury Alexander Hamilton issues his Report on Manufactures, which urged the government to develop a factory system.

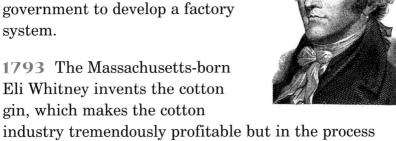

1793 The Massachusetts-born Eli Whitney invents the cotton gin, which makes the cotton industry tremendously profitable but in the process prolongs slavery.

1798 Eli Whitney builds a factory near New Haven, Connecticut, and begins to make muskets from inter-changeable parts; it marks the beginnings of mass production.

1802 Robert Fulton's steamship *Clermont* makes its first voyage.

1808 Oliver Evans builds a steam-powered flour mill in Pittsburgh, Pennsylvania.

1817 Work begins on the Erie Canal.

1830 A race between a horse and wagon and the train engine *Tom Thumb* is staged near Baltimore.

1844 Samuel Morse sends a telegraph message between Baltimore and Washington, D.C.

1851 Great Britain holds the Great Exhibition in London; many new devices of the Industrial Revolution are on display.

1861 The American Civil War begins.

1862 The battle between the *Monitor* and the *Merrimac*, two steam-powered ironclad ships, is fought in waters off Virginia and changes naval warfare forever.

1865 The Civil War ends.

1869 The transcontinental railroad is completed.

1877 A series of labor strikes against railroads and mines unsettles the U.S. public.

1886 The Centennial Exposition opens in Philadelphia and displays the latest steam engines and other machines; during the Haymarket riot in Chicago, four workers and eight police-men are killed.

1887 Congress creates the Interstate Commerce Commission, which has the power to regulate freight rates charged by railroads.

1889 The social reformer Jane Addams moves into Hull House.

1890 Jacob Riis publishes *How the Other Half Lives*, a shocking account of America's poor.

1893 The World Columbian Exposition opens in Chicago; the Panic of 1893 causes a nationwide depression.

1894 The Pullman Strike in Chicago results in a major railroad shutdown.

1901 Theodore Roosevelt becomes president and moves to break up giant companies called trusts.

1911 The Triangle Shirtwaist Fire in New York kills 146 workers, most of whom were young immigrant women; the tragic fire prompts laws to improve factory conditions.

1917 The United States enters World War I; a Communist revolution succeeds in Russia.

1924 Henry Ford reduces prices for his new cars and floods the market with automobiles.

1929 The U.S. stock market collapses, ushering in the Great Depression.

1933 President Franklin Roosevelt launches the New Deal, which is designed to provide depression relief.

1941 The United States enters World War II.

1945 The first atomic bomb is dropped on Hiroshima, Japan, bringing an end to World War II.

1950 A period of prosperity begins in the United States.

1960 The Industrial Revolution moves to Asia. By 2000, Asian countries produce most of the world's consumer goods.

Chapter Two   **Great Britain: Mother of the Industrial Revolution**

1. John Bowditch and Clement Ramsland, eds., *Voices of the Industrial Revolution* (Ann Arbor, Mich.: The University of Michigan Press, 1987), p. 129.
2. S.C. Burchell, *Age of Progress* (New York: Time-Life Books, 1966), p. 10.
3. Charles Dickens, *The Adventures of Oliver Twist* (New York: Oxford University Press, 1991), p. 35.
4. Sally Mitchell, *Daily Life in Victorian England* (London: Greenwood Press, 1996), pp. 43–44.
5. Bowditch and Ramsland, p. 86.

Chapter Three   **American Industrialization**

1. Gary Kornblith, ed., *The Industrial Revolution in America* (Boston: Houghton Mifflin Company, 1998), p. 3.
2. Allen Mandelbaum and Robert Richardson, eds., *Three Centuries of Poetry in America: 1620–1923* (New York: Bantam Books, 1999), p.171.
3. Alex Groner, *The American Heritage History of American Business and Industry* (New York: American Heritage Publishing Company, 1972), p. 60.
4. Margaret L. Coit, *Life History of the United States Volume Three 1789–1825: The Growing Years* (New York: Time-Life Books, 1974), p. 159.
5. Carl Sandburg, *The American Songbag* (New York: Harcourt Brace, 1927), p. 173.
6. Coit, p. 164.

7. Groner, p. 62.

8. Coit, p. 125.

Chapter Four **The Transformation of Life and Work**

1. Francis Russell, *The American Heritage History of the Confident Years* (New York: Bonanza Books, 1987), p. 159.

2. Carl Sandburg, *The American Songbag* (New York: Harcourt Brace, 1927), p. 367.

3. T. Harry Williams, *Life History of the United States Volume Six 1861–1876: The Union Restored* (New York: Time-Life Books, 1975), p. 165.

4. *Annals of America*, vol. 11 (Chicago: Encyclopedia Britannica, Inc., 1968), p. 355.

5. Ibid., vol. 12, p. 57.

6. "Table 4. Population: 1790–1990," *U.S. Census Bureau*, August 27, 1993, <http://www.census.gov/population/censusdata/table-4.pdf> (January 20, 2006).

7. Donald L. Miller, *City of the Century* (New York: Simon & Schuster, 1996), p. 218.

8. Bernard A. Weisberger, *Reaching For Empire* (New York: Time-Life Books, 1980), p. 74.

9. *Annals of America*, vol. 12, p. 220.

10. Ibid., vol. 11, pp. 197–198.

11. Ibid., p. 376.

12. Henry Steele Commanger, ed., *Witness to America* (New York: Barnes & Noble Books, 1996) pp. 956–957.

13. Page Smith, *The Rise of Industrial America: A*

People's History of the Post-Reconstruction Era, volume 6 (New York: McGraw-Hill, 1984), p. 218.

14. Ibid., p. 219.

Chapter Five   Tycoons and Toilers

1. Francis Russell, *The American Heritage History of the Confident Years* (New York: Bonanza Books, 1987), p. 234.

2. Page Smith, *The Rise of Industrial America: A People's History of the Post-Reconstruction Era* (New York: McGraw-Hill, 1984), p. 205.

3. Stephen Longstreet, *Chicago 1860–1919* (New York: David McKay Company, Inc., 1973), p. 427.

4. *Annals of America,* vol. 11 (Chicago: Encyclopedia Britannica, Inc., 1968), pp. 225–226.

5. John Bunyan, *"The Pilgrim's Progress,* p. 112," *Christian Classics Ethereal Library,* n.d., <http://www.ccel.org/ccel/bunyan/pilgrim.pdf> (January 20, 2006).

6. *Annals of America,* p. 291.

7. Upton Sinclair, *The Jungle* (New York: New American Library Edition, 1960), p. 43.

8. William Cahn, *A Pictorial History of American Labor* (New York: Crown Publishers, 1972), p. 143.

9. Samuel Eliot Morison, *History of the American People* (New York: Oxford University Press, 1965), p. 769

10. Smith, p. 245.

11. Ibid., p. 520.

12. Ibid., p. 521.

Chapter Six The Industrial Revolution in the Twentieth Century

1. *Annals of America*, vol. 12 (Chicago: Encyclopedia Britannica, Inc., 1968), p. 583.

3. Paul Le Blanc, *A Short History of the Working Class* (New York: Humanity Books, 1999), p. 66.

4. Edmund Stillman, *The American Heritage History of the 20's & 30's* (New York: Bonanza Books, 1987), p. 27.

5. Studs Terkel, *Hard Times: An Oral History of the Great Depression* (New York: Pantheon Books, 1970), p. 73.

Chapter Seven The Industrial Revolution Today

1. "The second industrial revolution," *BBC News*, May 11, 2004, <http://news.bbc.co.uk/1/hi/world/asia-pacific/3701581.stm> (October 11, 2005).

2. Ibid.

alloy—A mixture of metals.

anarchist—A person who believes in no form of government.

babble—Speech that is difficult or impossible to understand.

beguiling—Deceiving or mystifying.

ceremonious—Done with great celebration or fanfare.

chaos—Confusion or disorder.

cholera—An epidemic disease that is often fatal.

dexterous—Nimble in touch, a fine hand.

drudgery—Boring or tedious work.

entrepreneur—One who risks money to start a business.

gauging—Looking ahead to determine a future outcome.

militant—Highly determined in an almost military manner.

philanthropy—The practice of giving money to worthy causes.

squalid—Very dirty or unsightly.

symbol—One object or concept representing another.

typhus—A disease often caused by microorganisms.

Carson, Laurie. *Queen of Inventions: How the Sewing Machine Changed the World*. Milford, Conn.: Millbrook Press, 2003.

Collier, Christopher, and James Lincoln Collier. *The Rise of Industry: 1860–1900*. Tarrytown, N.Y.: Marshall Cavendish, 2000.

——— *The Rise of the Cities: 1820–1920*. Tarrytown, N.Y.: Marshall Cavendish, 2001.

Gunderson, Cory. *The Great Depression*. Edina, Minn.: ABDO, 2004.

Huff, Regan A. *Eli Whitney: The Cotton Gin and American Manufacturing*. New York: Rosen, 2004.

McKissack, Patricia, and Fred McKissack. *Booker T. Washington: Leader and Educator*. Berkeley Heights, N.J.: Enslow Publishers, Inc., 2001.

Pierce, Alan. *The Industrial Revolution*. Edina, Minn.: ABDO, 2005.

Pierce, Morris A. *Robert Fulton and the Development of Steamboats*. New York: Rosen, 2003.

Robinet, Harriette. *Missing from Haymarket Square*. New York: Simon & Schuster, 2001.

Woog, Adam. *A Sweatshop During the Industrial Revolution*. San Diego, Calif.: Lucent Books, 2003.

Industrial Revolution: America and the Industrial Revolution

Offers articles on important people of the period including Eli Whitney, Andrew Carnegie, and others.

<http://americanhistory.about.com>

Scroll down and click on "Industrial Revolution" at the left under "Topics."

Lesson: Industrial Revolution (Women in World History Curriculum)

Emphasizes the role of women in England and Wales during the early Industrial Revolution.

<http://www.womeninworldhistory.com>

Click on "Lessons" at the right. Scroll down and select "The Plight of Women's Work."

Reference Resources: Industrial Revolution

Highlights key people, places, and documents of the Industrial Revolution.

<http://www.kidinfo.com>

Click on the "Students" button. Select "American History." Click on "Industrial Revolution.